"You shall love the LORD your God with all your heart, and with all your soul, and with all your might. Keep these words that I am commanding to you today in your heart. Recite them to your children and talk about them when you are at home and when you are away, when you lie down and when you rise."

(Deuteronomy 6:5-7)

D0001890

Contents

How to Use
Celebrating Sunday for Catholic Families

This small weekly guide draws on the Gospel for each Sunday and Holyday for the coming year. It is intended to help parents engage their children with the Mass and deepen their appreciation of the richness of their faith life. So often, going to Mass becomes a weekly event that begins and ends at the church door. The brief reflection on an excerpt from the Gospel is intended to spark your thinking about the Scripture that will lead to conversation with your family before and after Mass. Suggestions for questions and conversation starters are provided, as well as some practice or practical way to carry this reflection into the life of the family. Keep in mind, however, that sometimes you may have other needs, concerns, or ideas that are more relevant to your home life at that moment. If so, engage your children with those.

Note that very young children are able to enter into the liturgy through their senses. Singing the hymns, calling their attention to the changing colors of the liturgical seasons, and sitting where they can observe the gestures of the Mass are all ways to form them in the faith. Always remember, as the rite of baptism proclaims, you, as parents, are your children's first and most important teachers. We hope that this book will enrich your family's life of faith.

September 5, 2021

Twenty-Third Sunday in Ordinary Time

Hearing the Word

Mark 7:31–37

In the name of the Father, and of the Son, and of the Holy Spirit.

Again Jesus left the district of Tyre, and went by way of Sidon to the Sea of Galilee, into the district of Decapolis. And people brought to him a deaf man who had a speech impediment and begged him to lay his hand on him. He took him off by himself away from the crowd. He put his finger into the man's ears and, spitting, touched his tongue; then he looked up to heaven and groaned, and said to him, *"Ephphatha!"*—that is, "Be opened!"—And immediately the man's ears were opened, his speech impediment was removed, and he spoke plainly. He ordered them not to tell anyone. But the more he ordered them not to, the more they proclaimed it. They were exceedingly astonished and they said, "He has done all things well. He makes the deaf hear and the mute speak."

Reflecting on the Word

In the work of creation, God brought the whole world into being. When Jesus opened the ears of the man and enabled him to speak, he created a whole new life for him.

The prophets foretold that when the Messiah comes the deaf would hear, the lame would leap, and the mute would sing (Isaiah 35:5–6). By the work of Jesus, people began to recognize him as the Savior they had been waiting for. He is the one who has come to bring us new life.

Sometimes we are deaf to words we need to hear and do not always speak the truth people need to hear. Let us ask Jesus to open our ears so we can hear his word and bless our tongues so we can speak his word.

......ON THE WAY TO MASS

How might we open ourselves up to everything that surrounds us—in the neighborhood, in the community of faith, in our own families? What might God be telling us?

ON THE WAY HOME FROM MASS ......

What do you think the man's first words were when he began to speak?

Living the Word

Do we pay attention to what God might be telling us? How do we make time to listen to him? Setting aside time for prayer as a family will help us be more open to listening to God and to proclaim the Gospel by the way we live.

September 12, 2021

Twenty-Fourth Sunday in Ordinary Time

Hearing the Word

Mark 8:27–35

In the name of the Father, and of the Son, and of the Holy Spirit.

Jesus and his disciples set out for the villages of Caesarea Philippi. Along the way he asked his disciples, "Who do people say that I am?" They said in reply, "John the Baptist, others Elijah, still others one of the prophets." And he asked them, "But who do you say that I am?" Peter said to him in reply, "You are the Christ." Then he warned them not to tell anyone about him.

He began to teach them that the Son of Man must suffer greatly and be rejected by the elders, the chief priests, and the scribes, and be killed, and rise after three days. He spoke this openly. Then Peter took him aside and began to rebuke him. At this he turned around and, looking at his disciples, rebuked Peter and said, "Get behind me, Satan. You are thinking not as God does, but as human beings do."

He summoned the crowd with his disciples and said to them, "Whoever wishes to come after me must deny himself, take up his cross, and follow me. For whoever wishes to save his life will lose it, but whoever loses his life for my sake and that of the gospel will save it."

Reflecting on the Word

What does it mean to be a disciple of Jesus Christ? If we acknowledge our belief that he is our Savior and choose to follow him, we must pick up our cross, whatever that may be. In order to have the strength to continue to follow Jesus we must pray that he may walk beside us on our path.

······ ON THE WAY TO MASS

Talk with your children about names: what do your teachers, friends, and family call you? While everyone may call you by your actual name, you may also be called by a nickname or a term of endearment. How do you feel when you are called by any of these names? Remember that you are also called a Christian. What feelings does that evoke in you?

ON THE WAY HOME FROM MASS ······

In addition to "Christ," Jesus has many other titles. We call him "Son of God," "the Light," "the Way," "the Good Shepherd," and "True Vine." How do these titles help you better understand who Jesus is? Which image of Jesus helps you to "take up your cross and follow" him, knowing he will support and protect you?

Living the Word

When we lose ourselves, we gain more trust and dependence on God. We gain more understanding, compassion, and wisdom toward others. As a family, decide how you can help ease the burden of people who suffer in your town or city. Or is there a friend or neighbor whose cross can be lighter if you help him or her carry it?

September 19, 2021

Twenty-Fifth Sunday in Ordinary Time

Hearing the Word

Mark 9:30–37

In the name of the Father, and of the Son, and of the Holy Spirit.

Jesus and his disciples left from there and began a journey through Galilee, but he did not wish anyone to know about it. He was teaching his disciples and telling them, "The Son of Man is to be handed over to men and they will kill him, and three days after his death the Son of Man will rise." But they did not understand the saying and they were afraid to question him.

They came to Capernaum and, once inside the house, he began to ask them, "What were you arguing about on the way?" But they remained silent. They had been discussing among themselves on the way who was the greatest. Then he sat down, called the Twelve, and said to them, "If anyone wishes to be first, he shall be the last of all and the servant of all." Taking a child, he placed it in their midst, and putting his arms around it, he said to them, "Whoever receives one child such as this in my name, receives me; and whoever receives me, receives not me but the One who sent me."

Reflecting on the Word

It is natural to want success and to accomplish or do something well. But how should we define success? Jesus gives us a wise way to measure it: he teaches us that greatness comes when we put ourselves at the service of others, just as he did throughout his life. Examples of greatness do not always appear in the places we expect. Jesus offered one example when he placed a child in the midst of the apostles. Let us look for examples of greatness among the least of us, the poor, the stranger, and even those who are the hardest to love.

······ ON THE WAY TO MASS

Ask your children, whom do you see as a leader? What have they done to show you this? What qualities do you think a leader should have?

ON THE WAY HOME FROM MASS ······

Why would the person who wishes to be first be last? Why would that person serve others? Recall the answers your children gave you on the qualities of leadership. Are they aligned with Jesus' definition of greatness?

Living the Word

Explain to your children what servant leadership means. Then invite each family member to name one person who is an example of service to others by what they say or do. What makes this person great and a servant to all? Say a prayer thanking God for these people who are great in the eyes of Jesus.

September 26, 2021

Twenty-Sixth Sunday in Ordinary Time

Hearing the Word

Mark 9:38–43, 45, 47–48

In the name of the Father, and of the Son, and of the Holy Spirit.

At that time, John said to Jesus, "Teacher, we saw someone driving out demons in your name, and we tried to prevent him because he does not follow us." Jesus replied, "Do not prevent him. There is no one who performs a mighty deed in my name who can at the same time speak ill of me. For whoever is not against us is for us. Anyone who gives you a cup of water to drink because you belong to Christ, amen, I say to you, will surely not lose his reward.

"Whoever causes one of these little ones who believe in me to sin, it would be better for him if a great millstone were put around his neck and he were thrown into the sea. If your hand causes you to sin, cut it off. It is better for you to enter into life maimed than with two hands to go into Gehenna, into the unquenchable fire. And if your foot causes you to sin, cut it off. It is better for you to enter into life crippled than with two feet to be thrown into Gehenna. And if your eye causes you to sin, pluck it out. Better for you to enter into the kingdom of God with one eye than with two eyes to be thrown into Gehenna, where 'their worm does not die, and the fire is not quenched.'"

Reflecting on the Word

The language in this Gospel is disturbing, almost frightening, but Jesus drives his point home. Nothing should distract or deter you from living the right way. The punishment for evil is separation from God forever. Nothing is worth that. The examples Jesus gives are extreme, but he speaks to encourage us to be careful about every action we take.

•••••• ON THE WAY TO MASS

What distracts or deters you from following Jesus? During the penitential rite, ask forgiveness for the times you didn't follow Jesus and ask for his help to stay on the straight path.

ON THE WAY HOME FROM MASS ••••••

What does it mean to follow Jesus? Is it easy or challenging? Whom can we turn to for help when we are tempted to stray from the straight path?

Living the Word

The gift of the sacrament of reconciliation is given to us as a way in which we can examine our lives in comparison to the life of Jesus and ask for help to do better. Consider celebrating this sacrament as a family soon.

October 3, 2021

Twenty-Seventh Sunday in Ordinary Time

Hearing the Word
Mark 10:2–9, 13–16

In the name of the Father, and of the Son, and of the Holy Spirit.

The Pharisees approached Jesus and asked, "Is it lawful for a husband to divorce his wife?" . . . He said to them in reply, "What did Moses command you?" They replied, "Moses permitted a husband to write a bill of divorce and dismiss her." But Jesus told them, "Because of the hardness of your hearts he wrote you this commandment. But from the beginning of creation, *God made them male and female. For this reason a man shall leave his father and mother and be joined to his wife, and the two shall become one flesh.* So they are no longer two but one flesh. Therefore what God has joined together, no human being must separate."

And people were bringing children to [Jesus] that he might touch them, but the disciples rebuked them. When Jesus saw this he became indignant and said to them, "Let the children come to me; do not prevent them, for the kingdom of God belongs to such as these. Amen, I say to you, whoever does not accept the kingdom of God like a child will not enter it." Then he embraced them and blessed them, placing his hands on them.

Reflecting on the Word

Jesus speaks about the beauty of marriage and the blessings that are the stronghold of the couple as they journey together through life. The holiness and grace within that act of commitment between two people can never be undone. Every day this commitment is a choice a family makes over and over again. Pope Francis wrote about families in "The Joy of Love" (*Amoris laetitia*), focusing on the joys and the challenges of married life. It is a wonderful message for all couples.

• • • • • • ON THE WAY TO MASS

Ask your children how they know that Jesus loves them. How does that love make them feel?

ON THE WAY HOME FROM MASS • • • • • •

Tell your children one way that each of them has brought you closer to God.

Living the Word

In today's Gospel, Jesus blessed the children that were brought to him. Remind your children that on the day of their baptism Jesus also blessed them with his light and life. Bless one another, using a sign from the baptismal rite. With your thumb, make a small sign of the cross on the forehead of the person next to you. Continue until each person has been blessed.

Twenty-Eighth Sunday in Ordinary Time

Hearing the Word

Mark 10:17–22

In the name of the Father, and of the Son, and of the Holy Spirit.

As Jesus was setting out on a journey, a man ran up, knelt down before him, and asked him, "Good teacher, what must I do to inherit eternal life?" Jesus answered him, "Why do you call me good? No one is good but God alone. You know the commandments: *You shall not kill; you shall not commit adultery; you shall not steal; you shall not bear false witness; you shall not defraud; honor your father and your mother.*" He replied and said to him, "Teacher, all of these I have observed from my youth." Jesus, looking at him, loved him and said to him, "You are lacking in one thing. Go, sell what you have, and give to the poor and you will have treasure in heaven; then come, follow me." At that statement his face fell and he went away sad, for he had many possessions.

Reflecting on the Word

We all know the commandments. We strive to honor our fathers and mothers and are faithful to keeping holy the Lord's day. But to sell all we have? To give all to the poor and follow the path of the cross? This challenge made the man walk away sadly. Our possessions can become the center of our existence and rob us of time and energy to enjoy our family, serve our community, and worship God. Listen to what God is asking of you. Let us ensure that our possessions do not get in the way of answering his call.

• • • • • • ON THE WAY TO MASS

Three of the commandments refer to our relationship with God. The other seven speak about our relationship with others. How many of the commandments can you name?

ON THE WAY HOME FROM MASS • • • • • •

Which commandment is the easiest to follow? The hardest to follow?

Living the Word

Where could you make more room for God in your life? Discuss what you could give up for a week to make space for God as a family together. Could you allot a time for service? Or pray the Rosary at night after dinner? Perhaps a weekend might be spent going through the house and reducing possessions. Talk together about the experience.

Twenty-Ninth Sunday in Ordinary Time

Hearing the Word

Mark 10:35–45

In the name of the Father, and of the Son, and of the Holy Spirit.

James and John, the sons of Zebedee, came to Jesus and said to him, "Teacher, we want you to do for us whatever we ask of you." He replied, "What do you wish me to do for you?" They answered him, "Grant that in your glory we may sit one at your right and the other at your left." Jesus said to them, "You do not know what you are asking. Can you drink the cup that I drink or be baptized with the baptism with which I am baptized?" They said to him, "We can." Jesus said to them, "The cup that I drink, you will drink and with the baptism with which I am baptized, you will be baptized; but to sit at my right or at my left is not mine to give but is for those for whom it has been prepared." When the ten heard this, they became indignant at James and John. Jesus summoned them and said to them, "You know that those who are recognized as rulers over the Gentiles lord it over them, and their great ones make their authority over them felt. But it shall not be so among you. Rather, whoever wishes to be great among you will be your servant; whoever wishes to be first among you will be the slave of all. For the Son of Man did not come to be served but to serve and to give his life as a ransom for many."

Reflecting on the Word

We parents spend much of our time taking care of our children. Sometimes it feels like we are sacrificing ourselves to give them everything they need. Jesus reminds us that we are imitating him when we serve, especially when it feels like we are giving our lives. Jesus gave himself freely. It was only because of his great love—for his Father and for us—that he was able to keep serving, keep giving. We must be sure our motives are pure and always based in love, that what we do is for God's glory only, and never for ours.

• • • • • • ON THE WAY TO MASS

The apostles James and John ask Jesus a favor. Ask your children, if you had the chance to ask Jesus a question what would it be?

ON THE WAY HOME FROM MASS • • • • • •

What do you think of the favor that James and John asked of Jesus? Do you think they really understood what they were asking?

Living the Word

This week, have your children take responsibility for serving the family meals. Go over a list of tasks, including helping to prepare food, setting the table, bringing food and drink to the table, and passing the dishes around to make sure everyone has had helpings of food or refreshing everyone's drinks. At the end of the week, talk about observations or lessons learned about service.

October 24, 2021

Thirtieth Sunday in Ordinary Time

Hearing the Word

Mark 10:46–52

In the name of the Father, and of the Son, and of the Holy Spirit.

As Jesus was leaving Jericho with his disciples and a sizable crowd, Bartimaeus, a blind man, the son of Timaeus, sat by the roadside begging. On hearing that it was Jesus of Nazareth, he began to cry out and say, "Jesus, son of David, have pity on me." And many rebuked him, telling him to be silent. But he kept calling out all the more, "Son of David, have pity on me." Jesus stopped and said, "Call him." So they called the blind man, saying to him, "Take courage; get up, Jesus is calling you." He threw aside his cloak, sprang up, and came to Jesus. Jesus said to him in reply, "What do you want me to do for you?" The blind man replied to him, "Master, I want to see." Jesus told him, "Go your way; your faith has saved you." Immediately he received his sight and followed him on the way.

Reflecting on the Word

Bartimaeus was a courageous man. He cried out to Jesus and placed his greatest need before him. Others tried to silence the man, yet Jesus answered his faith and courage with compassion. How courageous am I? Do I continue to ask God for what I need? Do I have faith that God will hear my request? Prayer is a wonderful way to put our needs before God and trust in God's love and care for us. The key to this passage is what the man did afterward. He followed Jesus "on the way," which was used to describe the early Christians. Are we "on the way"?

......ON THE WAY TO MASS

What is your greatest need today? When we pray the Prayer of the Faithful remember to silently add your request. Listen to and pray for all the other intentions.

ON THE WAY HOME FROM MASS ......

Which prayer of the faithful touched you today? How can you help make what we prayed for become a reality?

Living the Word

Our faith always seeks to understand the how and why of things. It is part of our human nature to use our reason. We do not want to be uninformed or blind to something. Allow your children to ask questions about the faith on any teachings they do not understand. Ask your pastor or director of catechesis or faith formation to recommend resources for your family.

October 31, 2021

Thirty-First Sunday in Ordinary Time

Hearing the Word

Mark 12:38b–34

In the name of the Father, and of the Son, and of the Holy Spirit.

One of the scribes came to Jesus and asked him, "Which is the first of all the commandments?" Jesus replied, "The first is this: *Hear, O Israel! The Lord our God is Lord alone! You shall love the Lord your God with all your heart, with all your soul, with all your mind, and with all your strength.* The second is this: *You shall love your neighbor as yourself.* There is no other commandment greater than these." The scribe said to him, "Well said, teacher. You are right in saying, 'He is One and there is no other than he.' And 'to love him with all your heart, with all your understanding, with all your strength, and to love your neighbor as yourself' is worth more than all burnt offerings and sacrifices." And when Jesus saw that he answered with understanding, he said to him, "You are not far from the kingdom of God." And no one dared to ask him any more questions.

Reflecting on the Word

Jesus says that when we understand these two great commandments we are not far from the kingdom of God. But it is also important to go beyond merely understanding to practicing them faithfully. How do I love God completely? Love of neighbor demands that we ask ourselves, "Who is my neighbor?" This is the work of a lifetime. When we try to live these tenets, we draw closer to God.

•••••• ON THE WAY TO MASS

Name one way to show love for God. Name one way to show love for other people.

ON THE WAY HOME FROM MASS ••••••

Today is All Hallows' Eve, the day before All Saints. This trio of days (Oct. 31–Nov. 2) calls our attention to those who have come before us in life and in faith. We especially remember those who have died. On All Souls' Day, *Día de los Muertos*, we remember and celebrate the lives and examples of their faith and love for us. Discuss how your family may honor your beloved dead and the saints who are special to you in the next couple of days.

Living the Word

Have your children cut out a large heart and write all the things they love on it. Cut the heart into pieces, with one item per piece. Then put the heart back together. Notice the cracks and how the heart doesn't hold its shape as well. Now make one big heart and write "God" on it. Paste the pieces in it to show that God holds everything.

November 7, 2021

Thirty-Second Sunday in Ordinary Time

Hearing the Word
Mark 12:38–44

In the name of the Father, and of the Son, and of the Holy Spirit.

In the course of his teaching Jesus said to the crowds, "Beware of the scribes, who like to go around in long robes and accept greetings in the marketplaces, seats of honor in synagogues, and places of honor at banquets. They devour the houses of widows and, as a pretext recite lengthy prayers. They will receive a very severe condemnation."

He sat down opposite the treasury and observed how the crowd put money into the treasury. Many rich people put in large sums. A poor widow also came and put in two small coins worth a few cents. Calling his disciples to himself, he said to them, "Amen, I say to you, this poor widow put in more than all the other contributors to the treasury. For they have all contributed from their surplus wealth, but she, from her poverty, has contributed all she had, her whole livelihood."

Reflecting on the Word

One of the most revered characters in Scripture is the poor widow who outshines us all with her profound generosity. She does not let her social status and her poverty keep her from contributing to the building of the kingdom of God. She gives all she has. She is our model. How can we develop the generous spirit of this poor widow? How can we become an example for others?

...... ON THE WAY TO MASS

Ask your children to think about why it is important to support our parish. How do they imagine the money is being used?

ON THE WAY HOME FROM MASS ......

The widow gave all that she had to the temple treasury. How does your family decide what to contribute to the support of the parish? Discuss the kinds of contributions each family member can make in terms of time, treasure, or talent.

Living the Word

Notice those who beg on our streets. They pose a challenge to us. How do we best help them? Do we give money, food coupons, bottled water, or a small snack? This is a good discussion to have with your family. Even if it doesn't lead to a final decision it helps us to focus on what, if any, is our commitment to contribute to these poor individuals. How do we put our decision into action?

November 14, 2021

Thirty-Third Sunday in Ordinary Time

Hearing the Word

Mark 13:24–32

In the name of the Father, and of the Son, and of the Holy Spirit.

Jesus said to his disciples: "In those days after that tribulation / the sun will be darkened, / and the moon will not give its light, / and the stars will be falling from the sky, / and the powers in the heavens will be shaken.

"And then they will see 'the Son of Man coming in the clouds' with great power and glory, and then he will send out the angels and gather his elect from the four winds, from the end of the earth to the end of the sky.

"Learn a lesson from the fig tree. When its branch becomes tender and sprouts leaves, you know that summer is near. In the same way, when you see these things happening, know that he is near, at the gates. Amen, I say to you, this generation will not pass away until all these things have taken place. Heaven and earth will pass away, but my words will not pass away.

"But of that day or hour, no one knows, neither the angels in heaven, nor the Son, but only the Father."

Reflecting on the Word

As we approach the end of the liturgical year, Mark's Gospel describes the end times. We are not sure when that time will come so we must ask ourselves, "Do we act as true followers of Jesus every day"? If we are faithful to our calling as Christians, we have nothing to fear. If your family participates in sports, music, or dance, or theater, you will know that you must prepare well in order to be ready. The same is true as we prepare ourselves to be with Jesus. What are some actions that help us to prepare?

• • • • • • ON THE WAY TO MASS

What dark events in the world frighten us today? What can we do to remind ourselves to rely on the help of Jesus? Do we pray for courage so that we can face any adversity?

ON THE WAY HOME FROM MASS • • • • • •

Invite each person to share how he or she prepares for the time when Jesus comes.

Living the Word

Write the word "PAROUSIA" in the center of a large sheet of drawing paper or card stock. Read 1 Corinthians 15:20–28 aloud to your children and explain that the Greek word *parousia* describes the time promised by Jesus when he will return in glory. What will the world be like when God is "all in all"? How will it be different from our lives now? Ask the children to draw what this might be like around the word "PAROUSIA."

Solemnity of Our Lord Jesus Christ, King of the Universe

Hearing the Word

John 18:33b–37

In the name of the Father, and of the Son, and of the Holy Spirit.

Pilate said to Jesus, "Are you the King of the Jews?" Jesus answered, "Do you say this on your own or have others told you about me?" Pilate answered, "I am not a Jew, am I? Your own nation and the chief priests handed you over to me. What have you done?" Jesus answered, "My kingdom does not belong to this world. If my kingdom did belong to this world, my attendants would be fighting to keep me from being handed over to the Jews. But as it is, my kingdom is not here." So Pilate said to him, "Then you are a king?" Jesus answered, "You say I am a king. For this I was born and for this I came into the world, to testify to the truth. Everyone who belongs to the truth listens to my voice."

Reflecting on the Word

This is the last Sunday of the liturgical year. We began the year last Advent by anticipating the birth of Jesus, our King. Today, at the end of the year, we celebrate Jesus as King of the Universe. Jesus admits that he is truly a king but one that Pontius Pilate does not understand. Take some time to reflect on the kingdom that Jesus announces and consider how you would describe the kind of king Jesus is.

......ON THE WAY TO MASS

When you think of a king and a kingdom what comes to mind? What does a good king do, say, and look like?

ON THE WAY HOME FROM MASS ......

Recall your discussion about kings and kingdoms. How does Jesus compare to the world's image of a king?

Living the Word

What does God expect of those who build his kingdom? Jesus says that everyone who belongs to the truth listens to his voice. How do we listen to his voice? How do we show that we belong to the truth? How do people in Jesus' kingdom speak to one another? How do they act toward one another? Then, as a family, decide how you will put this into practice.

November 28, 2021

First Sunday of Advent

Hearing the Word

Luke 21:25–28, 34–36

In the name of the Father, and of the Son, and of the Holy Spirit.

Jesus said to his disciples: "There will be signs in the sun, the moon, and the stars, and on earth nations will be in dismay, perplexed by the roaring of the sea and the waves. People will die of fright in anticipation of what is coming upon the world, for the powers of the heavens will be shaken. And then they will see the Son of Man coming in a cloud with power and great glory. But when these signs begin to happen, stand erect and raise your heads because your redemption is at hand.

"Beware that your hearts do not become drowsy from carousing and drunkenness and the anxieties of daily life, and that day catch you by surprise like a trap. For that day will assault everyone who lives on the face of the earth. Be vigilant at all times and pray that you have the strength to escape the tribulations that are imminent and to stand before the Son of Man."

Reflecting on the Word

At Mass, the priest asks us to bow our heads and pray for God's blessing. We genuflect when we enter the presence of the Blessed Sacrament in the tabernacle. We make a profound bow when the Word of God is presented to us. These gestures acknowledge our smallness before the greatness of God. Yet Jesus tells us we should raise our heads and stand before him at his second coming. Instead of dying of fright, we who have kept our baptismal light burning brightly can stand to greet our Lord because we know that, in his mercy, he is coming to redeem us.

......ON THE WAY TO MASS

What frightens you? How can we gain courage and strength from knowing that God is with us, that Jesus is beside us?

ON THE WAY HOME FROM MASS ......

Jesus reminds us to stay alert and be watchful. How can each of us be helpful reminders and good examples to do what is right and good?

Living the Word

The First Sunday of Advent is a good time to establish ways that your family can keep and honor the season of Advent. Does your family have an Advent wreath? Do you use an Advent calendar to count the days until Christmas? How will you prepare your heart as well as your home to receive the Christ child?

December 5, 2021

Second Sunday of Advent

Hearing the Word

Luke 3:1–6

In the name of the Father, and of the Son, and of the Holy Spirit.

In the fifteenth year of the reign of Tiberius Caesar, when
Pontius Pilate was governor of Judea, and Herod was tetrarch
of Galilee, and his brother Philip tetrarch of the region of
Ituraea and Trachonitis, and Lysanias was tetrarch of Abilene,
during the high priesthood of Annas and Caiaphas, the word
of God came to John the son of Zechariah in the desert. John
went throughout the whole region of the Jordan, proclaiming
a baptism of repentance for the forgiveness of sins, as it is
written in the book of the words of the prophet Isaiah: / *A voice
of one crying out in the desert: / "Prepare the way of the Lord, /
make straight his paths. / Every valley shall be filled / and every
mountain and hill shall be made low. / The winding roads shall
be made straight, / and the rough ways made smooth, / and all
flesh shall see the salvation of God."*

Reflecting on the Word

The birth of Jesus was not some abstract event. In fact, Jesus was born in a specific place at a specific time. We can locate his birth in history by identifying the leaders who lived at that time. Yet each year we prepare for Jesus to come into the world again, in our time. We must turn ourselves around to God and ask forgiveness of our sins.

......ON THE WAY TO MASS

John the Baptist called everyone to repentance. How can each of us help make our world ready to receive Jesus today?

ON THE WAY HOME FROM MASS ......

Many important people are named in today's Gospel. They correspond, in a way, to today's leaders. Who is the governor of your state? The bishop of your (arch)diocese? The priests and staff members in your parish? Like John the Baptist, we must continue to prepare the way for Jesus in our day and pray for our leaders that they do the same.

Living the Word

Are the preparations for Christmas overwhelming you or causing anxiety? Make time to gather as a family to reflect on how each member might spiritually prepare for Jesus' arrival. Ground your family in lasting things and do your best to ensure that materialism will not rule the day.

December 8, 2021

Solemnity of the Immaculate Conception of the Blessed Virgin Mary

Hearing the Word

Luke 1:26–38

In the name of the Father, and of the Son, and of the Holy Spirit.

The angel Gabriel was sent from God to a town of Galilee called Nazareth, to a virgin betrothed to a man named Joseph, of the house of David, and the virgin's name was Mary. And coming to her, he said, "Hail, full of grace! The Lord is with you." But she was greatly troubled at what was said and pondered what sort of greeting this might be. Then the angel said to her, "Do not be afraid, Mary, for you have found favor with God. Behold, you will conceive in your womb and bear a son, and you shall name him Jesus. He will be great and will be called Son of the Most High, and the Lord God will give him the throne of David his father, and he will rule over the house of Jacob forever, and of his Kingdom there will be no end." But Mary said to the angel, "How can this be, since I have no relations with a man?" And the angel said to her in reply, "The Holy Spirit will come upon you, and the power of the Most High will overshadow you. Therefore the child to be born will be called holy, the Son of God. And behold, Elizabeth, your relative, has also conceived a son in her old age, and this is the sixth month for her who was called barren; for nothing will be impossible for God." Mary said, "Behold, I am the handmaid

of the Lord. May it be done to me according to your word."
Then the angel departed from her.

Reflecting on the Word

God chose Mary from all women of all time to carry within
her and give birth to God as one of us. She did not know
exactly what would be required of her, but she trusted in
God and said yes. Thanks to Mary's cooperation with God's
plan, all of humanity is favored by the presence of the Lord,
a presence that will never end.

•••••• ON THE WAY TO MASS

What is something that would be hard for you to say yes to?

ON THE WAY HOME FROM MASS ••••••

What is God asking you to do today? Are you able to say yes,
even if you might feel unsure or afraid?

Living the Word

Do you know someone who is expecting a baby? Can you
do something to help her prepare? Many organizations
help young women who are expecting babies and have no
families to support them. Consider contributing to one of
these organizations to help a new baby begin life with hope.

December 12, 2021

THIRD SUNDAY OF ADVENT

Hearing the Word

Luke 3:10–18

In the name of the Father, and of the Son, and of the Holy Spirit.

The crowds asked John the Baptist, "What should we do?" He said to them in reply, "Whoever has two cloaks should share with the person who has none. And whoever has food should do likewise." Even tax collectors came to be baptized and they said to him, "Teacher, what should we do?" He answered them, "Stop collecting more than what is prescribed." Soldiers also asked him, "And what is it that we should do?" He told them, "Do not practice extortion, do not falsely accuse anyone, and be satisfied with your wages."

Now all the people were filled with expectation, and all were asking in their hearts whether John might be the Christ. John answered them all, saying, "I am baptizing you with water, but one mightier than I is coming. I am not worthy to loosen the thongs of his sandals. He will baptize you with the Holy Spirit and fire. His winnowing fan is in his hand to clear his threshing floor and to gather the wheat into his barn, but the chaff he will burn with unquenchable fire." Exhorting them in many other ways, he preached good news to the people.

Reflecting on the Word

It is interesting to note that John the Baptist never encouraged those who came to him to become someone or something different. He never told them to change occupations. He simply told them to be better at what they were already doing. Building God's kingdom, preparing others to recognize and receive Jesus in the world requires many different types of people and a variety of occupations and actions. We each have unique gifts to offer. It is also our responsibility to continue to improve and be better at what we do so we can contribute to the kingdom.

······ ON THE WAY TO MASS

Notice that the Advent candle this week is pink (rose). Why is it a different color today?

ON THE WAY HOME FROM MASS ······

Name the occupation of each member of your family, including student. Challenge your children to consider how John the Baptist would advise each family member in those occupations. In the context of those occupations, how would John answer?

Living the Word

The Third Sunday of Advent is also known as Gaudete Sunday. *Gaudete* means "joy." As a family member lights the third candle of your Advent wreath, rejoice in the warmth and joy of family. Invite them to pause each day this week to share something that brought them joy and to thank God for it.

December 19, 2021

Fourth Sunday of Advent

Hearing the Word

Luke 1:39–45

In the name of the Father, and of the Son, and of the Holy Spirit.

Mary set out and traveled to the hill country in haste to a town of Judah, where she entered the house of Zechariah and greeted Elizabeth. When Elizabeth heard Mary's greeting, the infant leaped in her womb, and Elizabeth, filled with the Holy Spirit, cried out in a loud voice and said, "Blessed are you among women, and blessed is the fruit of your womb. And how does this happen to me, that the mother of my Lord should come to me? For at the moment the sound of your greeting reached my ears, the infant in my womb leaped for joy. Blessed are you who believed that what was spoken to you by the Lord would be fulfilled."

Reflecting on the Word

Mary says yes in response to what God wants her to do. Then she immediately sets out on the way to become the bearer of Christ to others, by visiting her cousin Elizabeth. Elizabeth realizes who Mary is and what she is called to do because Mary was filled with the Holy Spirit. Let us pray that we might be filled with the Holy Spirit so that others may recognize us as Christ-bearers by the things we say and do.

······ ON THE WAY TO MASS

Recall a time when you traveled far to visit relatives. What was the journey like? How did it feel to finally arrive and see them?

ON THE WAY HOME FROM MASS ······

Does Elizabeth's response, "Blessed are you among women, and blessed is the fruit of your womb," sound familiar? What prayer includes these words?

Living the Word

After lighting the fourth candle on the Advent wreath, tell the family that today's Gospel story of the Visitation is the second of the five Joyful Mysteries of the Rosary. Explain that the other Joyful Mysteries are the Annunciation, the Nativity, the Presentation in the Temple, and the Finding of Jesus in the Temple. Ask your children why they think these are called the Joyful Mysteries. The other mysteries are called the Luminous, the Sorrowful, and the Glorious. Together, pray one Hail Mary or the Rosary.

December 26, 2021

Feast of the Holy Family of Jesus, Mary, and Joseph

Hearing the Word

Luke 2:41–52

In the name of the Father, and of the Son, and of the Holy Spirit.

Each year Jesus' parents went to Jerusalem for the feast of Passover, and when he was twelve years old, they went up according to festival custom. After they had completed its days, as they were returning, the boy Jesus remained behind in Jerusalem, but his parents did not know it. Thinking he was in the caravan, they journeyed for a day and looked for him among their relatives and acquaintances, but not finding him, they returned to Jerusalem to look for him. After three days they found him in the temple, sitting in the midst of the teachers, listening to them and asking them questions, and all who heard him were astounded at his understanding and his answers. When his parents saw him, they were astonished, and his mother said to him, "Son, why have you done this to us? Your father and I have been looking for you with great anxiety." And he said to them, "Why were you looking for me? Did you not know that I must be in my Father's house?" But they did not understand what he said to them. He went down with them and came to Nazareth, and was obedient to them; and his mother kept all these things in her heart. And Jesus advanced in wisdom and age and favor before God and man.

Reflecting on the Word

This is a wonderful story and one that resonates with every family. Children and teenagers can relate to sometimes being lost, physically or spiritually, and parents can relate to feeling anxiety and concern for their children. This story is also about the example that parents give to their children about their worship of God and about a child's realization that God's work can be done even by the very young. In the end, it is about the need for all of us to advance in wisdom, age, and grace with the help of God, no matter how old we are.

. . . . . . ON THE WAY TO MASS

Did you ever have the experience of being lost? Share your fears and your relief on being found.

ON THE WAY HOME FROM MASS . . . . . .

Why is it important to celebrate the Feast of the Holy Family? How are Jesus, Mary, and Joseph models for our home life?

Living the Word

The Bible does not tell us about Jesus' childhood, except to say that he grew in "wisdom and age and favor before God and man." To grow in wisdom, we always need to be open to learning new things. Perhaps your family can choose something to read or watch on television that will be a source of new information for all of you. Set aside a time to discuss what you have learned. It is also important to grow in grace. What new prayer experience can you share as a family?

Solemnity of the Epiphany of the Lord

Hearing the Word

Matthew 2:1–5, 7–12

In the name of the Father, and of the Son, and of the Holy Spirit.

When Jesus was born in Bethlehem of Judea, in the days of King Herod, behold, magi from the east arrived in Jerusalem, saying, "Where is the newborn king of the Jews? We saw his star at its rising and have come to do him homage." When King Herod heard this, he was greatly troubled, and all Jerusalem with him. Assembling all the chief priests and the scribes of the people, he inquired of them where the Christ was to be born. They said to him, "In Bethlehem of Judea. . . ." Then Herod called the magi secretly and ascertained from them the time of the star's appearance. He sent them to Bethlehem and said, "Go and search diligently for the child. When you have found him, bring me word, that I too may go and do him homage." After their audience with the king they set out. And behold, the star that they had seen at its rising preceded them, until it came and stopped over the place where the child was. They were overjoyed at seeing the star, and on entering the house they saw the child with Mary his mother. They prostrated themselves and did him homage. Then they opened their treasures and offered him gifts of gold, frankincense, and myrrh. And having been warned in a dream not to return to Herod, they departed for their country by another way.

Reflecting on the Word

The story of the Magi reminds us that the Christ child comes for all people. The Magi traveled from the ends of the earth led by the star to find Christ who is the Light of the world. They bring gifts that give us insight into who this newborn child is: gold for a king, incense for a priest, and myrrh for one who is to suffer.

• • • • • • ON THE WAY TO MASS

The Magi brought Jesus gold, frankincense, and myrrh. What gifts would you offer to the Christ child that express something about who *you* are and the talents *you* have?

ON THE WAY HOME FROM MASS • • • • • •

The word *epiphany* means "manifestation, revelation." What was revealed to the Magi? What revelations about God do you receive on this epiphany celebration?

Living the Word

In many parts of the world, this is a day for exchanging gifts. It is the twelfth day of Christmas, a day of celebration. Catholics traditionally mark the doorposts with the symbols 20+C+M+B+22. Each + symbol represents one of the four seasons, together connecting the year 2022 and the initials for the names of the Magi: Caspar, Melchior, and Balthazar. It is a reminder that we must welcome the traveler and all who enter through our doors and share what we have.

January 9, 2022

Feast of the Baptism of the Lord

Hearing the Word

Luke 3:15-16, 21-22

In the name of the Father, and of the Son, and of the Holy Spirit.

The people were filled with expectation, and all were asking in their hearts whether John might be the Christ. John answered them all, saying, "I am baptizing you with water; but one mightier than I is coming. I am not worthy to stoop and loosen the thongs of his sandals. He will baptize you with the Holy Spirit and fire."

After all the people had been baptized and Jesus also had been baptized and was praying, heaven was opened and the Holy Spirit descended upon him in a bodily form like a dove. And a voice came from heaven, "You are my beloved Son; with you I am well pleased."

Reflecting on the Word

The baptism of Jesus reminds each of us of our own baptism. The people gathered heard with words, "You are my beloved Son." At baptism, we are filled with the Holy Spirit and become beloved children of God. After his baptism, Jesus began his ministry to bring about the kingdom of God. Receiving God's own life has lit an unquenchable fire in us, God's beloved children, and kindled our desire to know God and tell others about him.

•••••• ON THE WAY TO MASS

As you enter church today, take special notice of the holy water font. Dip your fingers in the water and make a deliberate sign of the cross. Today's entry into the church is a reminder of the day you first became a member of the Christian community.

ON THE WAY HOME FROM MASS ••••••

Share a memory of your children's baptisms.

Living the Word

Many families keep and treasure the symbols of their baptisms. Continue your conversation by sharing pictures or video of each person's baptism, along with their candles and white garment, if you have them. Explain why each godparent was specially chosen. Tell your children about their names. Say a prayer of thanksgiving for being called to be a child of God.

January 16, 2022

SECOND SUNDAY IN ORDINARY TIME

Hearing the Word

John 2:1–11

In the name of the Father, and of the Son, and of the Holy Spirit.

There was a wedding at Cana in Galilee, and the mother of Jesus was there. Jesus and his disciples were also invited to the wedding. When the wine ran short, the mother of Jesus said to him, "They have no wine." And Jesus said to her, "Woman, how does your concern affect me? My hour has not yet come." His mother said to the servers, "Do whatever he tells you." Now there were six stone water jars there for Jewish ceremonial washings, each holding twenty to thirty gallons. Jesus told them, "Fill the jars with water." So they filled them to the brim. Then he told them, "Draw some out now and take it to the headwaiter." So they took it. And when the headwaiter tasted the water that had become wine, without knowing where it came from—although the servers who had drawn the water knew—, the headwaiter called the bridegroom and said to him, "Everyone serves good wine first, and then when people have drunk freely, an inferior one; but you have kept the good wine until now." Jesus did this as the beginning of his signs at Cana in Galilee and so revealed his glory, and his disciples began to believe in him.

Reflecting on the Word

This is a joyful story and one that tells us something important about who Jesus is. If you have ever been to a wedding, you know how much effort goes into preparing for it so the guests can enjoy the celebration. At Cana, the couple ran out of wine. Mary encouraged Jesus to help the couple and he responded to her request. The most important part of the story is revealed at the end. Jesus' action was a sign to the people around him that he was not just an ordinary person. This sign "revealed his glory," which is the glory of the one who sent him and to lead all to him.

•••••• ON THE WAY TO MASS

Recall a time when your family attended a wedding. Today's Gospel takes place at a wedding; listen carefully to what happens with Jesus.

ON THE WAY HOME FROM MASS ••••••

In the Gospel, we heard that Jesus changed the water into wine. At Mass, wine changes into something else. What do these signs mean?

Living the Word

Show your children your wedding photos or video. Talk to them about this commitment you made to family. Explain that this sacrament consecrates the entire family to God. Each family member is a sign of God's love at home and everywhere they go.

January 23, 2022

Third Sunday in Ordinary Time

Hearing the Word

Luke 4:14–21

In the name of the Father, and of the Son, and of the Holy Spirit.

Jesus returned to Galilee in the power of the Spirit, and news of him spread throughout the whole region. He taught in their synagogues and was praised by all.

He came to Nazareth, where he had grown up, and went according to his custom into the synagogue on the sabbath day. He stood up to read and was handed a scroll of the prophet Isaiah. He unrolled the scroll and found the passage where it was written: / *The Spirit of the Lord is upon me, / because he has anointed me / to bring glad tidings to the poor. / He has sent me to proclaim liberty to captives / and recovery of sight to the blind, / to let the oppressed go free, / and to proclaim a year acceptable to the Lord.* / Rolling up the scroll, he handed it back to the attendant and sat down, and the eyes of all in the synagogue looked intently at him. He said to them, "Today this Scripture passage is fulfilled in your hearing."

Reflecting on the Word

Jesus proclaims the passage he read from Isaiah "is fulfilled in your hearing." He declared himself to be chosen by God, the Messiah. Jesus began the work mentioned in Isaiah, but we know there is still more work to do. We are called to continue the work of Jesus. Jesus began this work in his hometown and spread to other towns. We can begin to spread God's Word among those who are close to us and, perhaps, one day share it with those who might be strangers and far away.

•••••• ON THE WAY TO MASS

Do you know anyone who is a reader at your parish? What is required of someone who wants to proclaim the Scriptures at Mass? One who proclaims the Scripture, like Jesus, must also be a living witness to them.

ON THE WAY HOME FROM MASS ••••••

Why is it important to listen to the readings at Mass?

Living the Word

In 2020, Pope Francis designated the Third Sunday in Ordinary Time as "Word of God Sunday." The pope encourages all of us to take some time today to read a passage of Scripture and reflect on its meaning in our own lives. Gather as a family today and choose a Scripture passage to proclaim and reflect on together. Then decide on how you will respond to God's Word.

January 30, 2022

Fourth Sunday in Ordinary Time

Hearing the Word

Luke 4:21–30

In the name of the Father, and of the Son, and of the Holy Spirit.

Jesus began speaking in the synagogue, saying: "Today this Scripture passage is fulfilled in your hearing." And all spoke highly of him and were amazed at the gracious words that came from his mouth. They also asked, "Isn't this the son of Joseph?" He said to them, "Surely you will quote me this proverb, 'Physician, cure yourself,' and say, 'Do here in your native place the things that we heard were done in Capernaum.'" And he said, "Amen, I say to you, no prophet is accepted in his own native place. Indeed, I tell you, there were many widows in Israel in the days of Elijah when the sky was closed for three and a half years and a severe famine spread over the entire land. It was to none of these that Elijah was sent, but only to a widow in Zarephath in the land of Sidon. Again, there were many lepers in Israel during the time of Elisha the prophet; yet not one of them was cleansed, but only Naaman the Syrian." When the people in the synagogue heard this, they were all filled with fury. They rose up, drove him out of the town, and led him to the brow of the hill on which their town had been built, to hurl him down headlong. But Jesus passed through the midst of them and went away.

Reflecting on the Word

Today's Gospel continues where last week's left off. Jesus had just read from the Scripture and declared that he was the one that the passage was referring to. Everyone who was listening knew Jesus and wondered how someone so ordinary could claim to be someone so great. The people became so angry with Jesus they wanted to throw him off a cliff! Jesus was admitting to who he truly was. Each one of us, as we reflect on God's Word, are called to be more than we already are: to grow as children of God and not be afraid to proclaim it.

......ON THE WAY TO MASS

Think about your gifts and talents. How are you using them to do God's work?

ON THE WAY HOME FROM MASS ......

Think about how Jesus' neighbors reacted to him. Are there times when trying to follow Jesus makes some of your friends angry with you? Do your actions challenge them?

Living the Word

Create acrostic poems that reflect your family's gifts and talents. Write a family member's name, one letter on each line, vertically on a sheet of paper. For each letter, choose descriptive words or phrases that best describe that person. Display the poems in your prayer space and let them be reminders of each person's gifts and talents. How will you support one another to use them to bring about the kingdom of God?

Fifth Sunday in Ordinary Time

Hearing the Word

Luke 5:4–11

In the name of the Father, and of the Son, and of the Holy Spirit.

[Jesus] said to Simon, "Put out into deep water and lower your nets for a catch." Simon said in reply, "Master, we have worked hard all night and have caught nothing, but at your command I will lower the nets." When they had done this, they caught a great number of fish and their nets were tearing. They signaled to their partners in the other boat to come to help them. They came and filled both boats so that the boats were in danger of sinking. When Simon Peter saw this, he fell at the knees of Jesus and said, "Depart from me, Lord, for I am a sinful man." For astonishment at the catch of fish they had made seized him and all those with him, and likewise James and John, the sons of Zebedee, who were partners of Simon. Jesus said to Simon, "Do not be afraid; from now on you will be catching men." When they brought their boats to the shore, they left everything and followed him.

Reflecting on the Word

Today's Gospel reminds us of the importance of two words: trust and humility. Simon and his coworkers put their trust in Jesus, followed his instructions and were rewarded with a huge catch of fish. Afterward, Simon felt unworthy to be in the presence of Jesus. But Jesus told him not to be afraid. Jesus had chosen Simon to do important work and he promised to be with him through it all. The same is true of us. We might feel that we are not always worthy followers of Jesus, yet Jesus trusts us to do the best we can. He trusts us to continue the work he began.

······ ON THE WAY TO MASS

Do you think God chooses a certain type of person to follow him?

ON THE WAY HOME FROM MASS ······

We heard today that God called fishermen to follow him. No matter who or what we are, we are all invited to be Jesus' disciples.

Living the Word

The right tools are needed to catch fish and people. What do you need to catch fish? You need a line, hooks, bobbers, sinkers, worms, lures, needle-nose pliers, a first-aid kit, sunscreen, a line cutter, a boat, and a fishing hat. What do you need to bring people to God? You need love, patience, and kindness, for a start. Ask your children to think of how they will share their faith with others this week.

February 13, 2022

Sixth Sunday in Ordinary Time

Hearing the Word

Luke 6:17, 20–23

In the name of the Father, and of the Son, and of the Holy Spirit.

Jesus came down with the Twelve and stood on a stretch of level ground with a great crowd of his disciples and a large number of the people from all Judea and Jerusalem and the coastal region of Tyre and Sidon. And raising his eyes toward his disciples he said: / "Blessed are you who are poor, / for the kingdom of God is yours. / Blessed are you who are now hungry, / for you will be satisfied. / Blessed are you who are now weeping, / for you will laugh. / Blessed are you when people hate you, / and when they exclude and insult you, / and denounce your name as evil / on account of the Son of Man. / Rejoice and leap for joy on that day! Behold, your reward will be great in heaven."

Reflecting on the Word

These beautiful statements are the Beatitudes, the blessings we receive when we act in the way presented in each one. These are not easy actions and attitudes to develop. They take a lifetime to perfect. But the promise Jesus makes is that our suffering will not be forever. We can look forward to wholeness, fulfillment, and joy with God forever.

••••••ON THE WAY TO MASS

How do you comfort someone who is sad? How do you help those who are poor and hungry?

ON THE WAY HOME FROM MASS ••••••

Which Beatitude do you most easily identify with? Why? Which Beatitude is the most challenging to live by? Why?

Living the Word

The Beatitudes appear twice in the New Testament. Luke sets this story with Jesus standing on level ground. In Matthew, however, this takes place on the top of a mountain. Read Matthew's version (5:1–12) and compare the two stories. What details do they have in common? How are they different? Why do you think the two are not exactly the same? (The evangelist Matthew wrote for a Jewish audience who would have understood that biblical events taking place on mountaintops were significant. They were moments to commune with God. Luke's audience were the early Christian communities.)

February 20, 2022

Seventh Sunday in Ordinary Time

Hearing the Word
Luke 6:27–36

In the name of the Father, and of the Son, and of the Holy Spirit.

Jesus said to his disciples: "To you who hear I say, love your enemies, do good to those who hate you, bless those who curse you, pray for those who mistreat you. To the person who strikes you on one cheek, offer the other one as well, and from the person who takes your cloak, do not withhold even your tunic. Give to everyone who asks of you, and from the one who takes what is yours do not demand it back. Do to others as you would have them do to you. For if you love those who love you, what credit is that to you? Even sinners love those who love them. And if you do good to those who do good to you, what credit is that to you? Even sinners do the same. If you lend money to those from whom you expect repayment, what credit is that to you? Even sinners lend to sinners, and get back the same amount. But rather, love your enemies and do good to them, and lend expecting nothing back; then your reward will be great and you will be children of the Most High, for he himself is kind to the ungrateful and the wicked. Be merciful, just as your Father is merciful."

Reflecting on the Word

These are challenging words and probably not easy ones for everyone to put into action. Jesus begins by setting apart those "who hear" from those who do not. Being Christian isn't easy because it means doing more than what we're comfortable with. We must be open to Jesus' words, not just the ones that make us comfortable, but especially those that make us uncomfortable. The difficult words of Jesus are the ones for which Jesus himself is our best example and model.

•••••• ON THE WAY TO MASS

Think of one person you have trouble getting along with. Pray for that person at church today. Then, beginning today, try to change the way you relate to that person.

ON THE WAY HOME FROM MASS ••••••

Does being compassionate and merciful make us weak? Does it mean we should let people take advantage of us? Or are we called to rise above pettiness and take the first step toward being as generous as God is?

Living the Word

Make a chart of Jesus' teachings in today's Gospel and challenge your family to practice these in the coming weeks. Display the chart in a prominent place or at your prayer table. Place a smiley-face sticker on the chart every time someone follows Jesus' teachings. See how many acts of kindness and love your family members can do!

Eighth Sunday in Ordinary Time

Hearing the Word

Luke 6:39–45

In the name of the Father, and of the Son, and of the Holy Spirit.

Jesus told his disciples a parable, "Can a blind person guide a blind person? Will not both fall into a pit? No disciple is superior to the teacher; but when fully trained, every disciple will be like his teacher. Why do you notice the splinter in your brother's eye, but do not perceive the wooden beam in your own? How can you say to your brother, 'Brother, let me remove that splinter in your eye,' when you do not even notice the wooden beam in your own eye? You hypocrite! Remove the wooden beam from your eye first; then you will see clearly to remove the splinter in your brother's eye.

"A good tree does not bear rotten fruit, nor does a rotten tree bear good fruit. For every tree is known by its own fruit. For people do not pick figs from thorn bushes, nor do they gather grapes from brambles. A good person out of the store of goodness in his heart produces good, but an evil person out of a store of evil produces evil; for from the fullness of the heart the mouth speaks."

Reflecting on the Word

In today's Gospel, Jesus uses two familiar images: a splinter/wooden beam and good/rotten fruit. It is easy for us to recognize the faults in others but be blind to our own. Jesus warns us not to judge too quickly. Our own faults may far outweigh the faults of others.

It is easy to identify the fruit an apple tree will produce. We know who and what a person is by how he or she acts or speaks. When we build up habits and attitudes based on love, we will grow more into the likeness of God.

......ON THE WAY TO MASS

What aspect of your life do you want to change? During the Penitential Rite, ask God's help to overcome your faults.

ON THE WAY HOME FROM MASS ......

It might be easier to recognize the bad in others, but it is healthier to identify what is good about them. Name one good quality in people you know.

Living the Word

Make a "fruit bowl" for your prayer table this week. Have your children use construction paper to cut shapes of fruit. Challenge them to think of ways the family can work on bearing good fruit, such as "praying at home," "donating a portion of allowance to the poor," "learning more about the saints," and so on. Each week, choose a fruit to work on together.

March 6, 2022

First Sunday of Lent

Hearing the Word

Luke 4:1–13

In the name of the Father, and of the Son, and of the Holy Spirit.

Filled with the Holy Spirit, Jesus returned from the Jordan and was led by the Spirit into the desert for forty days, to be tempted by the devil. He ate nothing during those days, and when they were over he was hungry. The devil said to him, "If you are the Son of God, command this stone to become bread." Jesus answered him, "It is written, *One does not live on bread alone.*" Then he took him up and showed him all the kingdoms of the world in a single instant. The devil said to him, "I shall give to you all this power and glory; for it has been handed over to me, and I may give it to whomever I wish. All this will be yours, if you worship me." Jesus said to him in reply, "It is written: / *You shall worship the Lord, your God, / and him alone shall you serve.*" / Then he led him to Jerusalem, made him stand on the parapet of the temple, and said to him, "If you are the Son of God, throw yourself down from here, for it is written: / *He will command his angels concerning you, to guard you, / and: / With their hands they will support you, / lest you dash your foot against a stone.*" / Jesus said to him in reply, "It also says, *You shall not put the Lord, your God, to the test.*" When the devil had finished every temptation, he departed from him for a time.

Reflecting on the Word

On the First Sunday of Lent, we always hear the story of Jesus' temptation in the desert. Jesus refused to give in to temptation. We must follow his example. Even when we read the last line "departed from him for a time," which tells us Jesus will be tempted again, we should not be discouraged. We will be tempted, too, but the same Spirit who led Jesus into the desert and helped him overcome temptation will be with us during times of temptation, and we can ask our Father to deliver us from evil.

......ON THE WAY TO MASS

Why are you sometimes tempted to do something you know is wrong? Remember you can rely on God's help to overcome it just as Jesus did.

ON THE WAY HOME FROM MASS ......

We will face the next forty days filled with temptations and challenges, just as Jesus did in the desert. The practices of Lent encourage us to pray more. How will you pray more so that you can avoid temptation?

Living the Word

The traditional Lenten practices are prayer, fasting, and almsgiving. When you remove, or fast from, certain things from your life you create space to introduce or expand others. What will you fast from this Lent? How will you give more to others in need? As a family, make a forty-day plan. At Easter, review what went well and what could have been better.

Second Sunday of Lent

Hearing the Word

Luke 9:28b–36

In the name of the Father, and of the Son, and of the Holy Spirit.

Jesus took Peter, John, and James and went up the mountain to pray. While he was praying his face changed in appearance and his clothing became dazzling white. And behold, two men were conversing with him, Moses and Elijah, who appeared in glory and spoke of his exodus that he was going to accomplish in Jerusalem. Peter and his companions had been overcome by sleep, but becoming fully awake, they saw his glory and the two men standing with him. As they were about to part from him, Peter said to Jesus, "Master, it is good that we are here; let us make three tents, one for you, one for Moses, and one for Elijah." But he did not know what he was saying. While he was still speaking, a cloud came and cast a shadow over them, and they became frightened when they entered the cloud. Then from the cloud came a voice that said, "This is my chosen Son; listen to him." After the voice had spoken, Jesus was found alone. They fell silent and did not at that time tell anyone what they had seen.

Reflecting on the Word

We hear the story of the Transfiguration every year on the Second Sunday of Lent. This year, we hear it from the evangelist Luke. The disciples were privileged to witness Jesus in his full glory on that mountaintop. These disciples will later accompany Jesus when he goes to the Garden of Olives to pray. Jesus is with us during challenging times and in joyful times.

······ON THE WAY TO MASS

Listen for familiar words in this Gospel. At what other time in Jesus' life do we hear a voice say, "This is my chosen Son; listen to him"? (We hear these words at Jesus' baptism.)

ON THE WAY HOME FROM MASS ······

Why do you think it was so important for God to announce to the disciples who Jesus is? Do you think it is a message just for Peter, John, and James?

Living the Word

Model for your child how you live as a disciple. Find an organization where you can serve with your child during Lent one week or more. Is your parish looking for liturgical ministers? Sign up to help during the Mass your family attends. Talk to your child about the importance of Christian discipleship and faith witnessing.

March 20, 2022

Third Sunday of Lent

Hearing the Word

Luke 13:1–9

In the name of the Father, and of the Son, and of the Holy Spirit.

Some people told Jesus about the Galileans whose blood Pilate had mingled with the blood of their sacrifices. Jesus said to them in reply, "Do you think that because these Galileans suffered in this way they were greater sinners than all other Galileans? By no means! But I tell you, if you do not repent, you will all perish as they did! Or those eighteen people who were killed when the tower at Siloam fell on them—do you think they were more guilty than everyone else who lived in Jerusalem? By no means! But I tell you, if you do not repent, you will all perish as they did!"

And he told them this parable: "There once was a person who had a fig tree planted in his orchard, and when he came in search of fruit on it but found none, he said to the gardener, 'For three years now I have come in search of fruit on this fig tree but have found none. So cut it down. Why should it exhaust the soil?' He said to him in reply, 'Sir, leave it for this year also, and I shall cultivate the ground around it and fertilize it; it may bear fruit in the future. If not you can cut it down.'"

Reflecting on the Word

The parables that Jesus used help us explore in many different ways the rich significance of Jesus' teachings. In the story of the fig tree, we can see ourselves. We are called to produce good fruit but sometimes we are not successful. However, we are not forsaken. The gardener advocates for mercy to allow the tree one more chance to produce good fruit. Jesus teaches that when we repent, and when we cultivate our relationship with God, we will bear fruit.

•••••• ON THE WAY TO MASS

God is merciful. Think of a time when you felt forgiven by God for something wrong you have done.

ON THE WAY HOME FROM MASS ••••••

If the fig tree in the Gospel represents us, who can the gardener be? How do you think the tree will respond to being allowed to grow once more?

Living the Word

As a family, schedule an educational visit to a greenhouse or botanical garden. Some questions to discuss with your children are: Why does a gardener need to prune plants to help them to stay healthy? What would a gardener do to cultivate the soil around a tree to help it to produce more fruit? How much patience must a gardener have to work with plants?

March 27, 2022

Fourth Sunday of Lent

Hearing the Word

Luke 15:11a, 13b, 14a, 14c, 20a, 20f–22a, 23b–24, 25, 28, 29, 31–32

In the name of the Father, and of the Son, and of the Holy Spirit.

[Jesus said]: "A man had two sons, . . . the younger son collected all his belongings and set off to a distant country where he squandered his inheritance on a life of dissipation. When he had freely spent everything, . . . he found himself in dire need. . . . Coming to his senses, . . . he got up and went back to his father. While he was still a long way off, his father . . . ran to his son, embraced him and kissed him. His son said to him, 'Father, I have sinned against heaven and against you; I no longer deserve to be called your son.' But his father ordered his servants, . . . 'Let us celebrate with a feast, because this son of mine was dead, and has come to life again; he was lost, and has been found.' Then the celebration began. Now the older son had been out in the field and, on his way back, as he neared the house, he heard the sound of music and dancing. . . . He became angry, and when he refused to enter the house, his father came out and pleaded with him. He said to his father in reply, 'Look, all these years I served you and not once did I disobey your orders; yet you never gave me even a young goat to feast on with my friends.' . . . [His father] said to him, 'My son you are here with me always; everything I have is yours. But now we must celebrate and rejoice, because your brother was dead and has come to life again; he was lost and has been found.'"

Reflecting on the Word

It is easy to think of ourselves as the good son. But the good son is also guilty of sin. He refuses to accept the goodness of the father. He considers his brother unworthy of their father's generosity and forgiveness. It is important to recognize and reflect on the action of the father who reaches out with love and mercy to both sons. He runs out to greet the younger son on the road, and he leaves the feast to bring the older son inside. Mercy and forgiveness are lessons that we all must learn.

......ON THE WAY TO MASS

Today's Gospel is a story about how a family relates to one another. How would you describe the relationships in your own family?

ON THE WAY HOME FROM MASS ......

After hearing the story of the prodigal son, which character do you relate to the most?

Living the Word

Lent is a good time to experience God's forgiveness and mercy in the sacrament of reconciliation. Before Easter, schedule a time for you and your older children to celebrate this sacrament. Children under the age of six do not understand the idea of sinning, so you might want to ask them to think of a time they did something wrong and you hugged them and kissed them. Explain that God is like a forgiving parent.

Fifth Sunday of Lent

Hearing the Word

John 8:3–11

In the name of the Father, and of the Son, and of the Holy Spirit.

The scribes and the Pharisees brought a woman who had been caught in adultery and made her stand in the middle. They said to him, "Teacher, this woman was caught in the very act of committing adultery. Now in the law, Moses commanded us to stone such women. So what do you say?" They said this to test him, so that they could have some charge to bring against him. Jesus bent down and began to write on the ground with his finger. But when they continued asking him, he straightened up and said to them, "Let the one among you who is without sin be the first to throw a stone at her." Again he bent down and wrote on the ground. And in response, they went away one by one, beginning with the elders. So he was left alone with the woman before him. Then Jesus straightened up and said to her, "Woman, where are they? Has no one condemned you?" She replied, "No one, sir." Then Jesus said, "Neither do I condemn you. Go, and from now on do not sin any more."

Reflecting on the Word

In today's Gospel, Jesus challenges us to look at our own failings before pointing out those of others. Jesus, who was without sin, set an example for us by not condemning the woman. Yet Jesus does not ignore the duty to exhort the woman to sin no more. We must pray for the grace to be forgiving of others. We must also be aware of times when we are tempted to sin and ask Jesus to be with us to help us resist.

......ON THE WAY TO MASS

Why is it so easy to criticize and condemn others?

ON THE WAY HOME FROM MASS ......

Instead of concentrating on others' faults and failings, can we try to identify with the person and have empathy? How is Jesus' action in today's Gospel a model of empathy and compassion?

Living the Word

The Pharisees in this Gospel talk about the law of Moses. Moses has given us the commandments of God that we are to follow. Together with your children, make a list of the Ten Commandments, discussing examples of how to obey each one. Make a plus sign next to the ones that are easy to obey and a negative sign next to the challenging ones. Choose one to work on this week and check in with the whole family on how well they are following the commandments.

April 10, 2022

Palm Sunday of the Passion of the Lord

Hearing the Word

Luke 19:36–40

In the name of the Father, and of the Son, and of the Holy Spirit.

As [Jesus] rode along, the people were spreading their cloaks on the road; and now as he was approaching the slope of the Mount of Olives, the whole multitude of his disciples began to praise God aloud with joy for all the mighty deeds they had seen. They proclaimed: / "Blessed is the king who comes / in the name of the Lord. / Peace in heaven / and glory in the highest."/ Some of the Pharisees in the crowd said to him, "Teacher, rebuke your disciples." He said in reply, "I tell you, if they keep silent, the stones will cry out!"

Reflecting on the Word

This is the first of two Gospel accounts proclaimed today, which focuses on the honor Jesus receives on his way into Jerusalem. The second will relate the story of Jesus' trial, passion, and death. The people cried out with praise and then some of the same people later cried out "crucify him." Aren't there times we praise God and other times when we refuse to follow in the way of Jesus? As we enter this Holy Week let us reflect on how we respond to Jesus.

······ ON THE WAY TO MASS

Listen for the words from the Gospel that are repeated in today's liturgy (Hosanna). We continue to join those who praise God with these words each time we worship together at Mass.

ON THE WAY HOME FROM MASS ······

Decide how the blessed palms will be displayed at home. Many families have a tradition of creating beautiful forms with the palms. How does your family use the palms as a sacramental?

Living the Word

This is the beginning of Holy Week, the most sacred time in our liturgical year. Look ahead at the schedule for prayer times and liturgies at your parish. Especially try to attend the Triduum services on Thursday, Friday, and Saturday. If there are people in your parish preparing for baptism at the Easter Vigil, keep them in your prayers every day this week.

April 17, 2022

Easter Sunday of the Resurrection of the Lord

Hearing the Word

John 20:1–9

In the name of the Father, and of the Son, and of the Holy Spirit.

On the first day of the week, Mary of Magdala came to the tomb early in the morning, while it was still dark, and saw the stone removed from the tomb. So she ran and went to Simon Peter and to the other disciple whom Jesus loved, and told them, "They have taken the Lord from the tomb, and we don't know where they put him." So Peter and the other disciple went out and came to the tomb. They both ran, but the other disciple ran faster than Peter and arrived at the tomb first; he bent down and saw the burial cloths there, but did not go in. When Simon Peter arrived after him, he went into the tomb and saw the burial cloths there, and the cloth that had covered his head, not with the burial cloths but rolled up in a separate place. Then the other disciple also went in, the one who had arrived at the tomb first, and he saw and believed. For they did not yet understand the Scripture that he had to rise from the dead.

Reflecting on the Word

Alleluia! Today, we celebrate the heart of our Christian faith: that God's life and love are stronger than death. Mary, Peter, and John "did not yet understand . . . that [Jesus] had to rise from the dead." Keep in mind how shocking this event must have been for Mary and the disciples. But though they did not fully understand, they believed, as we do today. We are filled with the promise of God's life. This is cause for great rejoicing!

......ON THE WAY TO MASS

Ask your children to take notice of any signs of new life in nature. What once appeared dead is now full of life.

ON THE WAY HOME FROM MASS ......

We will continue to celebrate Easter Time over the next fifty days until the Solemnity of Pentecost. At home, use a bright yellow marker to count each day on a calendar beginning with today up to and including June 5, the Solemnity of Pentecost. Explain to your children that the bright yellow color reminds us of Jesus, our Light.

Living the Word

It is a tradition in many families to color eggs for Easter. Eggs are a wonderful symbol of new life. They also remind us of how Jesus' tomb was broken open to reveal new life. Use some of your colored eggs to make a beautiful centerpiece for your table today.

April 24, 2022

Second Sunday of Easter / Sunday of Divine Mercy

Hearing the Word

John 20:19–29

In the name of the Father, and of the Son, and of the Holy Spirit.

On the evening of that first day of the week, when the doors were locked, where the disciples were, . . . Jesus came and stood in their midst and said to them, "Peace be with you." When he had said this, he showed them his hands and his side. The disciples rejoiced when they saw the Lord. Jesus said to them again, "Peace be with you. As the Father has sent me, so I send you." And when he had said this, he breathed on them and said to them, "Receive the Holy Spirit. Whose sins you forgive are forgiven them, and whose sins you retain are retained."

Thomas, called Didymus, one of the Twelve, was not with them when Jesus came. So the other disciples said to him, "We have seen the Lord." But he said to them, "Unless I see the mark of the nails in his hands and put my finger into the nailmarks and put my hand into his side, I will not believe."

Now a week later . . . Jesus came . . . and said, "Peace be with you." Then he said to Thomas, "Put your finger here and see my hands, and bring your hand and put it into my side, and do not be unbelieving, but believe." Thomas answered and said to him, "My Lord and my God!" Jesus said to him, "Have you come to believe because you have seen me? Blessed are those who have not seen and have believed."

Reflecting on the Word

When Jesus says, "Blessed are those who have not seen and have believed," he could be talking about you and me. We did not walk and talk and eat with Jesus. Those who did bore witness to him and shared their experiences with others. This was passed on from generation to generation to the present time. One quality that marks us as believers is how we are an instrument of God's mercy. Do we show others compassion and love?

......ON THE WAY TO MASS

The Second Sunday of Easter is also known as the Sunday of Divine Mercy. How are peace and mercy related?

ON THE WAY HOME FROM MASS ......

Is there anyone who needs our forgiveness and mercy? Ask God to soften your heart and show others mercy through your actions and words.

Living the Word

Together, learn more about St. Faustina, who helped spread this devotion. The image of the Sacred Heart was a focus of her prayer. The image of "Divine Mercy" shows the love of Jesus radiating out of his heart toward all people. Research that image and ask your children to talk about what they see.

May 1, 2022

Third Sunday of Easter

Hearing the Word

John 21:1–9, 12, 15–17

In the name of the Father, and of the Son, and of the Holy Spirit.

At that time, Jesus revealed himself again to his disciples . . . . Together were Simon Peter, Thomas called Didymus, Nathanael . . . Zebedee's sons, and two others of his disciples. Simon Peter said to them, "I am going fishing." They said to him, "We also will come with you." . . . When it was already dawn, Jesus was standing on the shore; . . . "Children, have you caught anything to eat?" They answered him, "No." So he said to them, "Cast the net over the right side of the boat and you will find something." So they cast it, and were not able to pull it in because of the number of fish. So the disciple whom Jesus loved said to Peter, "It is the Lord." When Simon Peter heard that it was the Lord, . . . [he] jumped into the sea. The other disciples came in the boat . . . dragging the net with the fish. When they climbed out on shore, . . . Jesus said to them, "Come, have breakfast." . . .

When they had finished breakfast, Jesus said to Simon Peter, "Simon, son of John, do you love me more than these?" Simon Peter answered him, "Yes, Lord, you know that I love you." Jesus said to him, "Feed my lambs." He then said to Simon Peter a second time, "Simon, son of John, do you love me?" Simon Peter answered him, "Yes, Lord, you know that I love you." Jesus said to him, "Tend my sheep." Jesus said to him the third time, "Simon, son of John, do you love me?" Peter was distressed that Jesus had said to him a third time, "Do you love me?" and he said to him, "Lord you know everything; you know that I love you." Jesus said to him, "Feed my sheep."

Reflecting on the Word

The first time that Jesus called Peter to follow him was when he was fishing. Jesus told Peter he would make him a fisher of men. Now, after the resurrection, Jesus again visits Peter on the shore while he is fishing. Jesus gives Peter a mission to feed the people who will follow him. Only one thing is necessary for this task, that Peter love Jesus. Out of his love for Jesus will yield everything he needs to be faithful to his mission. The same is true for us if we choose to follow Jesus and care for his lambs and sheep. We must do it out of love.

......ON THE WAY TO MASS

Jesus called ordinary working people to follow him and do his work. Peter was a fisherman. What are the occupations of people you know who follow Jesus? How do their occupations help promote the kingdom of God?

ON THE WAY HOME FROM MASS ......

Why did Jesus ask Peter three times if he loved him? What do you think Jesus meant when he said, "Feed my lambs and sheep"?

Living the Word

All the groups advertised in your parish bulletin support your parish. Your support of these advertisers helps them in turn. What other actions that may have gone unnoticed contribute to the working of your parish?

May 8, 2022

Fourth Sunday of Easter

Hearing the Word

John 10:27–30

In the name of the Father, and of the Son, and of the Holy Spirit.

Jesus said, "My sheep hear my voice; I know them, and they follow me. I give them eternal life, and they shall never perish. No one can take them out of my hand. My Father, who has given them to me, is greater than all, and no one can take them out of the Father's hand. The Father and I are one."

Reflecting on the Word

The Fourth Sunday of Easter is also known as Good Shepherd Sunday. Each year we hear from a different evangelist who gives us a different perspective of the Good Shepherd. This year we hear that the sheep hear the voice of Jesus. At our baptism, we become part of the Good Shepherd's sheepfold. He personally calls us by name and knows us completely. Like the sheep, we live in community, and we all belong to God.

· · · · · · ON THE WAY TO MASS

Today is Mother's Day. Besides your mother, think of one other person in your life who is like a shepherd. Who watches over you? Cares for you? Keeps you safe? Pray especially for that person and your mother at Mass.

ON THE WAY HOME FROM MASS · · · · · ·

Who are really the sheep that Jesus refers to? Are they just the people you know, your family and friends? Could they include the people you don't know, in your neighborhood, town, and country? Could they be people from all nationalities and religions? Every human being is part of the family of God.

Living the Word

The parable of the Good Shepherd helps very young children know and fall in love with Jesus. Helping them form this relationship is foundational to their spiritual development. Read John 10:11, 14–16 and Psalm 23. Reflect together without preaching to your children and listen to their responses.

May 15, 2022

Fifth Sunday of Easter

Hearing the Word

John 13:31–33a, 34–35

In the name of the Father, and of the Son, and of the Holy Spirit.

When Judas had left them, Jesus said, "Now is the Son of Man glorified, and God is glorified in him. If God is glorified in him, God will also glorify him in himself, and God will glorify him at once. My children, I will be with you only a little while longer. I give you a new commandment: love one another. As I have loved you, so you also should love one another. This is how all will know that you are my disciples, if you have love for one another."

Reflecting on the Word

"Love one another." One simple sentence contains the heart of all Jesus teachings. More than that, Jesus says we are to love others as he loves us. Jesus lived his whole life in service to others. At the Last Supper, he gave us a model by washing the feet of his disciples and telling them to follow his example. We each have different gifts and we are called to use those gifts in the service of others. That is how we love as Jesus loved.

● ● ● ● ● ● ON THE WAY TO MASS

How do you know you are really loved? How do you show other people how much you love them?

ON THE WAY HOME FROM MASS ● ● ● ● ● ●

What gifts and talents have we been blessed with that will help us act with love?

Living the Word

Ask your children to recall their gifts and talents. Provide them with red construction paper, pens and markers, and scissors. Help them to cut out a dozen little hearts. On each heart, have them write one way they can use their talents to show God's love to one another. Place all the hearts in small box or basket to place on your prayer table. Each day, pray over the hearts and then choose one. Help one another to act upon that task. After this activity has been completed, discuss whether these actions helped each become stronger disciples of Jesus.

May 22, 2022

Sixth Sunday of Easter

Hearing the Word

John 14:23–29

In the name of the Father, and of the Son, and of the Holy Spirit.

Jesus said to his disciples: "Whoever loves me will keep my word, and my Father will love him, and we will come to him and make our dwelling with him. Whoever does not love me does not keep my words; yet the word you hear is not mine but that of the Father who sent me.

"I have told you this while I am with you. The Advocate, the Holy Spirit whom the Father will send in my name, will teach you everything and remind you of all that I told you. Peace I leave with you; my peace I give to you. Not as the world gives do I give it to you. Do not let your hearts be troubled or afraid. You heard me tell you, 'I am going away and I will come back to you.' If you loved me, you would rejoice that I am going to the Father; for the Father is greater than I. And now I have told you this before it happens, so that when it happens you may believe."

Reflecting on the Word

"Peace I leave with you." Jesus didn't mean the peace we know in the world, an absence of war. The peace of Jesus is a share in the life of God that grounds us, surrounds us, comforts us, and allows us to be one with others. What a precious gift this is! Not only are we promised peace, but also that God will dwell in us if we keep the word of Jesus. At our baptism, we became children of God, now it is up to us to maintain that relationship by keeping God's word and God's law.

••••••ON THE WAY TO MASS

During the exchange of peace at Mass today, be intentional about sharing your peace. Look the other person in the eyes and say, "Peace be with you," or use your own words.

ON THE WAY HOME FROM MASS ••••••

Many things disturb us in our lives. One source of strength can be found in the words of Jesus, "Do not let your hearts be troubled or afraid." Are you able to turn your anxieties over to God?

Living the Word

Reflect on how you are a peacemaker in your community. How do you spread peace to and with others? When do you fall short of being an active peacemaker? As a family, volunteer at a local peacemaking organization. Pray that that your family will always be able to rest secure in the peace of Christ.

May 29, 2022

Solemnity of the Ascension of the Lord / Seventh Sunday of Easter

Hearing the Word

Luke 24:46–53

In the name of the Father, and of the Son, and of the Holy Spirit.

Jesus said to his disciples: "Thus it is written that the Christ would suffer and rise from the dead on the third day and that repentance, for the forgiveness of sins, would be preached in his name to all the nations, beginning from Jerusalem. You are witnesses of these things. And behold I am sending the promise of my Father upon you; but stay in the city until you are clothed with power from on high."

Then he led them out as far as Bethany, raised his hands, and blessed them. As he blessed them he parted from them and was taken up to heaven. They did him homage and then returned to Jerusalem with great joy, and they were continually in the temple praising God.

Reflecting on the Word

Before Jesus returned to his Father in heaven, he spoke to his disciples and called them witnesses to all they had seen and heard. A witness is someone who speaks the truth about certain events. A good witness can be believed. Jesus wanted his disciples to tell everyone the truth about his life and death.

We were not with Jesus, but we have learned about him from those who have gone before us in faith. Now it becomes our responsibility to be witnesses.

......ON THE WAY TO MASS

The Ascension of the Lord commemorates Jesus leaving the apostles and going home to the Father in heaven. Recall a time when a friend or classmate moved away. How did you feel when that person left?

ON THE WAY HOME FROM MASS ......

What does it mean to be a witness to the Christian faith?

Living the Word

Jesus' ascension was, in some ways, a starting point for the Christian missionary activity throughout the world. This week, do research online on worldwide Catholic missionary organizations. Educate yourself about the work that they do around the globe and the many challenges that they face and share what you find with your children. Pray for these people, along with those they serve, especially those who are in dangerous and life-threatening locales.

June 5, 2022

Solemnity of Pentecost

Hearing the Word

John 14:15–16, 23b–26

In the name of the Father, and of the Son, and of the Holy Spirit.

Jesus said to his disciples: "If you love me, you will keep my commandments. And I will ask the Father, and he will give you another Advocate to be with you always.

"Whoever loves me will keep my word, and my Father will love him, and we will come to him and make our dwelling with him. Those who do not love me do not keep my words; yet the word you hear is not mine but that of the Father who sent me.

"I have told you this while I am with you. The Advocate, the Holy Spirit whom the Father will send in my name will teach you everything and remind you of all that I told you."

Reflecting on the Word

In today's Gospel, the Holy Spirit is called the "Advocate."
An advocate is one who stands up for and defends another.
It is someone who pleads or speaks on another's behalf.
Jesus tells us the Father sends the Holy Spirit to speak on
Jesus' behalf and to help us remember what he has taught.
The Spirit also pleads on our behalf before God as we struggle
to live God's Word.

......ON THE WAY TO MASS

Do you ever pray to the Holy Spirit?

ON THE WAY HOME FROM MASS ......

What comes to mind when you think about the Holy Spirit?

Living the Word

Part of the Pentecost story is that once the Holy Spirit
came upon the disciples, they were able to understand each
other despite the different languages they were all speaking.
In how many languages can the members of your family tell
one another, "I love you"? Look it up in a different language
every day this week and share it with one another.

June 12, 2022

Solemnity of the Most Holy Trinity

Hearing the Word

John 16:12–15

In the name of the Father, and of the Son, and of the Holy Spirit.

Jesus said to his disciples: "I have much more to tell you, but you cannot bear it now. But when he comes, the Spirit of truth, he will guide you to all truth. He will not speak on his own, but he will speak what he hears, and will declare to you the things that are coming. He will glorify me, because he will take from what is mine and declare it to you. Everything that the Father has is mine; for this reason I told you that he will take from what is mine and declare it to you."

Reflecting on the Word

The Holy Spirit guided the apostles and early Church in reflecting on the mystery of Trinity and continues to unfold this mystery for us. It will take lifetimes to fully understand the mystery of the Trinity. But we can begin by viewing the Trinity through the lens of relationship. The Father, Son, and Holy Spirit are in relationship with one another. We are invited to be a part of that relationship, too.

• • • • • • ON THE WAY TO MASS

Each time we enter church we are reminded of our baptism and the Trinity. Be attentive when you dip your hand in the holy water font and sign yourself with the cross, praying, "In the name of the Father, and of the Son and of the Holy Spirit. Amen."

ON THE WAY HOME FROM MASS • • • • • •

Which Person of the Trinity do you relate to the most: the Father, the Son, or the Holy Spirit? Why?

Living the Word

You can find many digital resources about faith online. This week, do a search for images about the Trinity with your children. This is a great way to see classic and contemporary representations of the Trinity, which can help spark your reflections on this holy mystery of our faith.

June 19, 2022

Solemnity of the Most Holy Body and Blood of Christ

Hearing the Word

Luke 9:11b–17

In the name of the Father, and of the Son, and of the Holy Spirit.

Jesus spoke to the crowds about the kingdom of God, and he healed those who needed to be cured. As the day was drawing to a close, the Twelve approached him and said, "Dismiss the crowd so that they can go to the surrounding villages and farms and find lodging and provisions; for we are in a deserted place here." He said to them, "Give them some food yourselves." They replied, "Five loaves and two fish are all we have, unless we ourselves go and buy food for all these people." Now the men there numbered about five thousand. Then he said to his disciples, "Have them sit down in groups of about fifty." They did so and made them all sit down. Then taking the five loaves and the two fish, and looking up to heaven, he said the blessing over them, broke them, and gave them to the disciples to set before the crowd. They all ate and were satisfied. And when the leftover fragments were picked up, they filled twelve wicker baskets.

Reflecting on the Word

The story of the loaves and fishes reminds us that Jesus always has enough to nourish and satisfy us. We will never be left hungry if we trust in the one who gives us his own Body and Blood. As we approach the table of the Lord, we know we will be filled with all good things. Jesus fills us up so that we can share him with others. The twelve wicker baskets remind us that there is always an overflow of love in the sacred food we receive.

......ON THE WAY TO MASS

Today is Father's Day when we celebrate and honor those men in our lives who take care of us and provide us with what we need to live a good life. Say a prayer to express your love and gratitude for the men who show you God's love and care.

ON THE WAY HOME FROM MASS ......

Why is it important to come to Mass and receive Holy Communion?

Living the Word

As a family, volunteer to help at the local food pantry or participate in a meal distribution program. Many parishes have onsite sandwich-making programs to benefit those in need. Explain to your children that these projects will enable your family to share the abundance of God's blessings with other people in our human family.

June 26, 2022

Thirteenth Sunday in Ordinary Time

Hearing the Word

Luke 9:51–62

In the name of the Father, and of the Son, and of the Holy Spirit.

When the days for Jesus' being taken up were fulfilled, he resolutely determined to journey to Jerusalem, and he sent messengers ahead of him. On the way they entered a Samaritan village to prepare for his reception there, but they would not welcome him because the destination of his journey was Jerusalem. When the disciples James and John saw this they asked, "Lord, do you want us to call down fire from heaven to consume them?" Jesus turned and rebuked them, and they journeyed to another village.

As they were proceeding on their journey someone said to him, "I will follow you wherever you go." Jesus answered him, "Foxes have dens and birds of the sky have nests, but the Son of Man has nowhere to rest his head."

And to another he said, "Follow me." But he replied, "Lord, let me go first and bury my father." But he answered him, "Let the dead bury their dead. But you, go and proclaim the kingdom of God." And another said, "I will follow you, Lord, but first let me say farewell to my family at home." To him Jesus said, "No one who sets a hand to the plow and looks to what was left behind is fit for the kingdom of God."

Reflecting on the Word

This is a difficult reading and an even more difficult challenge. Jesus calls us to follow him—without hesitation or exception. Sometimes we respond to God's call like the person who says, "I will . . . but first . . . ." We put conditions on our discipleship. We may practice our faith but only when it is convenient. Total commitment is difficult. We can only hope to be successful because Jesus has gone before us to show us the way. We must walk in his footsteps and pray for his help.

•••••• ON THE WAY TO MASS

What kind of person do you think leaves everything to follow Jesus? What do you think it means to leave everything behind?

ON THE WAY HOME FROM MASS ••••••

Have you sometimes put something else before God? Reflect on the reasons why. What are some reasons why we hesitate to commit fully to following Jesus? How can we overcome these hesitations?

Living the Word

The path of discipleship is one that requires the disciple to make sacrifices to truly follow Jesus. At the end of each Mass, the presider or deacon tells us to go out into the world and live our lives according to the Gospel. Pray about what that means in your lives. What sacrifices can you make to respond properly to your baptismal call of discipleship?

July 3, 2022

Fourteenth Sunday in Ordinary Time

Hearing the Word

Luke 10:1–12

In the name of the Father, and of the Son, and of the Holy Spirit.

At that time the Lord appointed seventy-two others whom he sent ahead of him in pairs to every town and place he intended to visit. He said to them, "The harvest is abundant but the laborers are few; so ask the master of the harvest to send out laborers for his harvest. Go on your way; behold, I am sending you like lambs among wolves. Carry no money bag, no sack, no sandals; and greet no one along the way. Into whatever house you enter, first say, 'Peace to this household.' If a peaceful person lives there, your peace will rest on him; but if not, it will return to you. Stay in the same house and eat and drink what is offered to you, for the laborer deserves his payment. Do not move about from one house to another. Whatever town you enter and they welcome you, eat what is set before you, cure the sick in it and say to them, 'The kingdom of God is at hand for you.' Whatever town you enter and they do not receive you, go out into the streets and say, 'The dust of your town that clings to our feet, even that we shake off against you.' Yet know this: the kingdom of God is at hand. I tell you, it will be more tolerable for Sodom on that day than for that town."

Reflecting on the Word

Jesus charges his followers with a great task. At the outset of their journey he warns them of many dangers and yet tells them to take very little with them. They are to rely on God and the goodness of the people they serve. Some people will respond to their preaching, while others will not. That should not be their concern. They are only called to be faithful to the task set before them and let God do the rest.

• • • • • • ON THE WAY TO MASS

When you have something big or important to do, is it easier to have a helper? Why or why not?

ON THE WAY HOME FROM MASS • • • • • •

What do you feel you are being called to do in order to help bring about God's kingdom? Name three things. Would you enlist helpers for those tasks?

Living the Word

We are called to help build God's kingdom and we are also citizens who are charged with building a country that sees all people as equal and provides them with what they need for life and liberty. As we celebrate Independence Day, let us ask God's blessings on our country, its leaders, and citizens. May we be a light to the world and a blessing to all those who struggle or are oppressed.

July 10, 2022

Fifteenth Sunday in Ordinary Time

Hearing the Word

Luke 10:30–35

In the name of the Father, and of the Son, and of the Holy Spirit.

[Jesus said,] "A man fell victim to robbers as he went down from Jerusalem to Jericho. They stripped and beat him and went off leaving him half-dead. A priest happened to be going down that road, but when he saw him, he passed by on the opposite side. Likewise a Levite came to the place, and when he saw him, he passed by on the opposite side. But a Samaritan traveler who came upon him was moved with compassion at the sight. He approached the victim, poured oil and wine over his wounds and bandaged them. Then he lifted him up on his own animal, took him to an inn, and cared for him. The next day he took out two silver coins and gave them to the innkeeper with the instruction, 'Take care of him. If you spend more than what I have given you, I shall repay you on my way back.'"

Reflecting on the Word

This Scripture passage is so familiar it requires our careful attention so that we don't overlook its message. The Samaritan who approached the victim was not a friend or a neighbor. So why did he stop when others didn't? Because he was "moved with *compassion*," which means "to suffer with." The Samaritan saw his own vulnerability in another human being who was suffering and tried to ease that suffering.

......ON THE WAY TO MASS

Who do I know is suffering today? Remember to include them in your prayers, especially at the Prayers of the Faithful.

ON THE WAY HOME FROM MASS ......

How do you define *neighbor* in the context of today's Gospel?

Living the Word

Consider borrowing the book *The Three Questions* by Jon J. Muth from the library and read it together with your family. It is a children's book based on a story by Leo Tolstoy that asks three questions: When is the best time to do things? Who is the most important one? What is the right thing to do? Many adults feel uncomfortable or unsure of what to do when confronted with people begging for money. Your children are likely learning from your behavior. Whether it's giving money when you are asked or donating regularly to a shelter, decide on your means for helping the homeless, model it consistently, and communicate it to your children.

July 17, 2022

Sixteenth Sunday in Ordinary Time

Hearing the Word

Luke 10:38–42

In the name of the Father, and of the Son, and of the Holy Spirit.

Jesus entered a village where a woman whose name was Martha welcomed him. She had a sister named Mary who sat beside the Lord at his feet listening to him speak. Martha, burdened with much serving, came to him and said, "Lord, do you not care that my sister has left me by myself to do the serving? Tell her to help me." The Lord said to her in reply, "Martha, Martha, you are anxious and worried about many things. There is need of only one thing. Mary has chosen the better part and it will not be taken from her."

Reflecting on the Word

Martha and Mary were both very close friends of Jesus. They were sisters but they had very different personalities. Jesus loved them both. Jesus does not chastise Martha's hospitality or attention to detail but her inability to be present with him in the moment. On the other hand, Mary's trust in Jesus allowed her to be at peace and listen to the words Jesus spoke. Let us not let the work and worries of our lives keep us from the treasure of Jesus' words.

●●●●●● ON THE WAY TO MASS

The time that we dedicate to worship is the time that we sit at the feet of Jesus, in peace, and listen to his words. Pay special attention during Mass, especially during the Liturgy of the Word. Be at peace like Mary.

ON THE WAY HOME FROM MASS ●●●●●●

Who are you more like, Martha or Mary? Have you ever been too busy for God? Do you take time for prayer or Scripture reflection?

Living the Word

We all face a new week when school, work, and other responsibilities will all vie for our time. We will encounter issues and experiences that will make us anxious and worried. As a family, comfort one another by praying together each day, at mealtime or bedtime. Pray for yourselves and for one another. Give God thanks for the blessings of this day and ask for God's help to face the next day.

Seventeenth Sunday in Ordinary Time

Hearing the Word

Luke 11:1–13

In the name of the Father, and of the Son, and of the Holy Spirit.

Jesus was praying in a certain place, and when he had finished, one of his disciples said to him, "Lord, teach us to pray just as John taught his disciples." He said to them, "When you pray, say: / Father, hallowed be your name, / your kingdom come. / Give us each day our daily bread / and forgive us our sins / for we ourselves forgive everyone in debt to us, / and do not subject us to the final test."

And he said to them, "Suppose one of you has a friend to whom he goes at midnight and says, 'Friend, lend me three loaves of bread, for a friend of mine has arrived at my house from a journey and I have nothing to offer him,' and he says in reply from within, 'Do not bother me; the door has already been locked and my children and I are already in bed. I cannot get up to give you anything.' I tell you, if he does not get up to give the visitor the loaves because of their friendship, he will get up to give him whatever he needs because of his persistence.

"And I tell you, ask and you will receive; seek and you will find; knock and the door will be opened to you. For everyone who asks, receives; and the one who seeks, finds; and to the one who knocks, the door will be opened. What father among you would hand his son a snake when he asks for a fish? Or hand him a scorpion when he asks for an egg? If you then, who are wicked, know how to give good gifts to your children, how much more will the Father in heaven give the Holy Spirit to those who ask him?"

Reflecting on the Word

Jesus himself taught us to approach God as Father. Each of these examples demonstrate how generous God is. They encourage us to trust in God to hear our needs and respond. We must never tire of expressing our needs in prayer. Let us be certain that we ask for what is right—what we need and not just what we want.

・・・・・・ON THE WAY TO MASS

Pay careful attention to the Our Father during Mass today. Jesus is teaching us that God loves us as a parent and responds to our needs. Pray with confidence as children of a God who loves us.

ON THE WAY HOME FROM MASS ・・・・・・

Think of one phrase from the Our Father that stands out to you. Explain why.

Living the Word

Talk candidly at home about your prayer life this week. When have you prayed? When have you felt that your prayers were answered? Were your prayers ever answered in a way that you weren't expecting? Just as Jesus learned to pray from his mother, Mary, your children will learn to pray from you.

July 31, 2022

Eighteenth Sunday in Ordinary Time

Hearing the Word

Luke 12:13–21

In the name of the Father, and of the Son, and of the Holy Spirit.

Someone in the crowd said to Jesus, "Teacher, tell my brother to share the inheritance with me." He replied to him, "Friend, who appointed me as your judge and arbitrator?" Then he said to the crowd, "Take care to guard against all greed, for though one may be rich, one's life does not consist of possessions."

Then he told them a parable. "There was a rich man whose land produced a bountiful harvest. He asked himself, 'What shall I do, for I do not have space to store my harvest?' And he said, 'This is what I shall do: I shall tear down my barns and build larger ones. There I shall store all my grain and other goods and I shall say to myself, "Now as for you, you have so many good things stored up for many years, rest, eat, drink, be merry!"' But God said to him, 'You fool, this night your life will be demanded of you; and the things you have prepared, to whom will they belong?' Thus will it be for all who store up treasure for themselves but are not rich in what matters to God."

Reflecting on the Word

The rich man in the parable acted wisely. He worked hard to produce a good harvest and planned to store it for his future. This sounds like he is being prudent. However, we must always be mindful of producing good works in the eyes of God and storing those up, not for ourselves but for the good of all those around us. We must produce good fruit. We do so by remaining close to God. Let us pray that God guide us to make good decisions this week.

•••••• ON THE WAY TO MASS

What is the difference between needing something and wanting it? How often do you really need the things that you want?

ON THE WAY HOME FROM MASS ••••••

Did the rich man act in a bad way? What did he neglect to think about as he did his work?

Living the Word

Sometimes siblings have a hard time sharing their things with others. This week, ask each family member to pay attention to all the sharing that goes on in the house. When they see it, have them call out, "Thank you for sharing!" This will show cooperation and how sharing helps to develop a happy and healthy home environment. Talk about how, if people learn how to share in their homes, they will be more able to know how to share in the world.

Nineteenth Sunday in Ordinary Time

Hearing the Word

Luke 12:32–40

In the name of the Father, and of the Son, and of the Holy Spirit.

Jesus said to his disciples: "Do not be afraid any longer, little flock, for your Father is pleased to give you the kingdom. Sell your belongings and give alms. Provide money bags for yourself that do not wear out, an inexhaustible treasure in heaven that no thief can reach nor moth destroy. For where your treasure is, there also will your heart be.

"Gird your loins and light your lamps and be like servants who await their master's return from a wedding, ready to open immediately when he comes and knocks. Blessed are those servants whom the master finds vigilant on his arrival. Amen, I say to you, he will gird himself, have them recline at table, and proceed to wait on them. And should he come in the second or third watch and find them prepared in this way, blessed are those servants. Be sure of this: if the master of the house had known the hour when the thief was coming, he would not have let his house be broken into. You also must be prepared, for at an hour you do not expect, the Son of Man will come."

Reflecting on the Word

We are told to be prepared, and to choose wisely what we desire as our treasure. Then Jesus gives us a unique reason for these actions. So often, Jesus calls us to be servants. In this passage, however, the good servants are waited on by the Master. What a turnabout! If we prepare ourselves well and make good choices in our lifetimes we will be rewarded greatly when we are with God. Because no one knows when Jesus will return, we must always be prepared. We cannot rest from our duties as Christians.

• • • • • • ON THE WAY TO MASS

What do you treasure most? (Think about where we put all our effort and desire.)

ON THE WAY HOME FROM MASS • • • • • •

Recall what each person treasures the most. Think about them in the context of today's Gospel. Do the things we treasure help us to be prepared for when Jesus comes?

Living the Word

The servants in the Gospel watched as they waited for the master so that they could help him whenever he arrived. People usually don't plan to need help. This week, practice being observant of the needs of others—at school, work, or home. As a family, discuss what you noticed and how you responded.

August 14, 2022

Twentieth Sunday in Ordinary Time

Hearing the Word

Luke 12:49–53

In the name of the Father, and of the Son, and of the Holy Spirit.

Jesus said to his disciples: "I have come to set the earth on fire, and how I wish it were already blazing! There is a baptism with which I must be baptized, and how great is my anguish until it is accomplished! Do you think that I have come to establish peace on the earth? No, I tell you, but rather division. From now on a household of five will be divided, three against two and two against three; a father will be divided against his son and a son against his father, a mother against her daughter and a daughter against her mother, a mother-in-law against her daughter-in- law and a daughter-in-law against her mother-in-law."

Reflecting on the Word

It might seem alarming to some that Jesus says that he came to bring division, not peace. Jesus is talking about the cost of doing the will of God. He speaks of accomplishing something great—the realization of God's kingdom—and doing so with the kind of passion and fortitude that might harm our relationships with others. Others might have lukewarm responses to discipleship, an attitude that could cause rifts and conflicts. Jesus challenges us to continue his work and make this our highest priority.

•••••• ON THE WAY TO MASS

Tell your children that they might hear some confusing or disturbing words in the Gospel today. Reassure them that you will discuss them later.

ON THE WAY HOME FROM MASS ••••••

Ask your children what questions they have about today's Gospel. Discuss whether they think that Jesus wants families to be divided. Why could his message have that effect?

Living the Word

We hold up saints as examples of those who followed Christ unconditionally. Some saints suffered ridicule, cruelty, and even death at the hands of family members because of the path they chose. Research a saint who was persecuted by his or her family. Some examples are St. Francis of Assisi, St. Clare, St. Thomas Aquinas, St. Elizabeth Ann Seton, and St. Kateri Tekakwitha. Discuss their responses in light of today's Gospel.

August 21, 2022

Twenty-First Sunday in Ordinary Time

Hearing the Word
Luke 13:22–30

In the name of the Father, and of the Son, and of the Holy Spirit.

Jesus passed through towns and villages, teaching as he went and making his way to Jerusalem. Someone asked him, "Lord, will only a few people be saved?" He answered them, "Strive to enter through the narrow gate, for many, I tell you, will attempt to enter but will not be strong enough. After the master of the house has arisen and locked the door, then will you stand outside knocking and saying, 'Lord, open the door for us.' He will say to you in reply, 'I do not know where you are from.' And you will say, 'We ate and drank in your company and you taught in our streets.' Then he will say to you, 'I do not know where you are from. Depart from me, all you evil-doers!' And there will be wailing and grinding of teeth when you see Abraham, Isaac and Jacob and all the prophets in the kingdom of God and you yourselves cast out. And people will come from the east and the west and from the north and the south and will recline at table in the kingdom of God. For behold, some are last who will be first, and some are first who will be last."

Reflecting on the Word

The people in this passage plead with Jesus, offering their faithfulness as a reason for being saved. They ate and drank and listened to Jesus as he spoke among them. Yet Jesus answers by saying he does not know them. What is lacking? We, too, share in the sacred meal at Eucharist. We listen to the Word of God proclaimed in our churches. What else are we challenged to do in order to "be saved"? In addition to prayer, Mass, and the sacraments, serving others will bring us closer to God.

• • • • • • ON THE WAY TO MASS

At every Eucharist, we are invited to share the sacred meal of Christ's Body and Blood. How does receiving the Eucharist prepare us to live as Jesus teaches us?

ON THE WAY HOME FROM MASS • • • • • •

The kingdom of God requires an active engagement on our part. How can we be more intentional about what we say or do?

Living the Word

If your parish has scheduled Eucharistic adoration, that would be an ideal opportunity to show your children how we honor the real presence of Christ in the host. During adoration, show your children how to genuflect before the monstrance.

August 28, 2022

Twenty-Second Sunday in Ordinary Time

Hearing the Word

Luke 14:1, 7–14

In the name of the Father, and of the Son, and of the Holy Spirit.

On a sabbath Jesus went to dine at the home of one of the leading Pharisees.

He told a parable to those who had been invited, noticing how they were choosing the places of honor at the table. "When you are invited by someone to a wedding banquet, do not recline at table in the place of honor. A more distinguished guest than you may have been invited by him, and the host who invited both of you may approach you and say, 'Give your place to this man,' and then you would proceed with embarrassment to take the lowest place. Rather, when you are invited, go and take the lowest place so that when the host comes to you he may say, 'My friend, move up to a higher position.' Then you will enjoy the esteem of your companions at the table. For everyone who exalts himself will be humbled, but the one who humbles himself will be exalted." Then he said to the host who invited him, "When you hold a lunch or a dinner, do not invite your friends or your brothers or your relatives or your wealthy neighbors, in case they may invite you back and you have repayment. Rather, when you hold a banquet, invite the poor, the crippled, the lame, the blind; blessed indeed will you be because of their inability to repay you. For you will be repaid at the resurrection of the righteous."

Reflecting on the Word

Jesus challenges us to know our rightful place by practicing humility. Being humble means being able to recognize who we truly are and act out of that understanding. We must judge ourselves neither to be too great nor too small.

We must also learn to give freely. It is easy to be generous to our friends. How can we expand our generosity to include those who are beyond that circle?

• • • • • • ON THE WAY TO MASS

When I am with a group of people—in school, at work, with friends—do I always seek to be first? When we give expecting a return, is that truly being generous?

ON THE WAY HOME FROM MASS • • • • • •

How can we be generous to others we don't know?

Living the Word

Be mindful of how your words match your actions this week. When you promise to do something for a family member, coworker, or classmate, make sure your actions follow your words. Let people know by your kind or loving actions that you are a disciple of Jesus. No words are necessary when doing a good deed for someone in need.

EVERYDAY FAMILY PRAYERS

The Sign of the Cross

The Sign of the Cross is the first prayer and the last—of each day, and of each Christian life. It is a prayer of the body as well as a prayer of words. When we are presented for baptism, the community traces this sign on our bodies for the first time. Parents may trace it daily on their children. We learn to trace it daily on ourselves and on those whom we love. When we die, our loved ones will trace this holy sign on us for the last time.

In the name of the Father,

and of the Son,

and of the Holy Spirit. Amen.

The Lord's Prayer

The Lord's Prayer, or the Our Father, is a very important prayer for Christians because Jesus himself taught it to his disciples, who taught it to his Church. Today, we say this prayer as part of Mass, in the Rosary, and in personal prayer. There are seven petitions in the Lord's Prayer. The first three ask for God to be glorified and praised, and the next four ask for God to help take care of our physical and spiritual needs.

Our Father, who art in heaven,

hallowed be thy name;

thy kingdom come,

thy will be done

on earth as it is in heaven.

Give us this day our daily bread,

and forgive us our trespasses,

as we forgive those who trespass against us;

and lead us not into temptation, but deliver us from evil.

The Apostles' Creed

The Apostles' Creed is one of the earliest creeds we have; scholars believe it was written in the second century. The Apostles' Creed is shorter than the Nicene Creed, but it states what we believe about the Father, Son, and Holy Spirit. This prayer is sometimes used at Mass, especially at Masses with children, and is part of the Rosary.

I believe in God,

the Father almighty,

Creator of heaven and earth,

and in Jesus Christ, his only Son, our Lord,

who was conceived by the Holy Spirit,

born of the Virgin Mary,

suffered under Pontius Pilate,

was crucified, died and was buried;

he descended into hell;

and on the third day he rose again from the dead;

he ascended into heaven,

and is seated at the right hand of God the Father almighty;

from there he will come to judge the living and the dead.

I believe in the Holy Spirit,

the holy catholic Church,

the communion of saints,

the forgiveness of sins,

the resurrection of the body,

and life everlasting. Amen.

The Nicene Creed

The Nicene Creed was written at the Council of Nicaea in AD 325, when bishops of the Church gathered together in order to articulate true belief in who Christ is and in his relationship to God the Father. The Nicene Creed was the final document of that Council, written so that all the faithful may know the central teachings of Christianity. We say this prayer at Mass.

I believe in one God,

the Father almighty,

maker of heaven and earth,

of all things visible and invisible.

I believe in one Lord Jesus Christ,

the Only Begotten Son of God,

born of the Father before all ages.

God from God, Light from Light,

true God from true God,

begotten, not made, consubstantial with the Father;

through him all things were made.

For us men and for our salvation

he came down from heaven,

and by the Holy Spirit was incarnate of the Virgin Mary,

and became man.

For our sake he was crucified under Pontius Pilate,
he suffered death and was buried,
and rose again on the third day
in accordance with the Scriptures.
He ascended into heaven
and is seated at the right hand of the Father.
He will come again in glory
to judge the living and the dead
and his kingdom will have no end.

I believe in the Holy Spirit, the Lord, the giver of life,
who proceeds from the Father and the Son,
who with the Father and Son is adored and glorified,
who has spoken through the prophets.

I believe in one holy, catholic, and apostolic Church.
I confess one Baptism for the forgiveness of sins
and I look forward to the resurrection of the dead
and the life of the world to come. Amen.

Glory Be (Doxology)

This is a short prayer that Christians sometimes add to the end of psalms. It is prayed during the Rosary and usually follows the opening verse during the Liturgy of the Hours. It can be prayed at any time during the day.

Glory be to the Father

and to the Son

and to the Holy Spirit,

as it was in the beginning

is now, and ever shall be

world without end. Amen.

Hail Mary

The first two lines of this prayer are the words of the angel Gabriel to Mary, when he announces that she is with child (Luke 1:28). The second two lines are Elizabeth's greeting to Mary (Luke 1:42). The last four lines come to us from deep in history, from where and from whom we do not know. This prayer is part of the Rosary and is often used by Christians for personal prayer.

Hail, Mary, full of grace,

the Lord is with thee.

Blessed art thou among women

and blessed is the fruit of thy womb, Jesus.

Holy Mary, Mother of God,

pray for us sinners,

now and at the hour of our death.

Amen.

Grace before Meals

Families pray before meals in different ways. Some families make up a prayer in their own words, other families sing a prayer, and many families use this traditional formula. Teach your children to say this prayer while signing themselves with the cross.

Bless us, O Lord, and these thy gifts,

which we are about to receive from thy bounty,

through Christ our Lord.

Amen.

Grace after Meals

Teach your children to say this prayer after meals, while signing themselves with the cross. The part in brackets is optional.

We give thee thanks, for all thy benefits,

almighty God, who lives and reigns forever.

[And may the souls of the faithful departed,

through the mercy of God, rest in peace.]

Amen.